T0271157

The Employee and the Post-Pandemic Workplace

The UN Sustainable Development Goals, an increasing interest in Environmental, Social and Governance factors, and the unprecedented impact of the COVID-19 pandemic have triggered a massive change in how companies and employees view their relationship, the role and meaning of work, and how to adapt to new environments and ways of working. This book covers a key topic for companies and management practice – that of how to create and foster a committed workforce in a post-pandemic era that has seen a radical change in working environments, approaches and employee understanding of her/his career and work-life balance.

In this book, leading researchers and practitioners in the field of CSR, management, leadership, and human resources from the schools and corporate partners of the Council on Business & Society provide the latest focuses on the workplace post-pandemic, effectively managing virtual teams, collective and responsible leadership, and insights into policies and processes enhancing employee commitment and performance. Each insight is accompanied by key takeaways, food for thought and further reading, and later followed by microcase studies.

This accessible book will be a valuable resource for scholars, instructors, and upper-level students across leadership and human resource management-related disciplines, enabling them to synthesise the knowledge presented for their own context (professional, academic, personal, wider society, and the planet).

Adrián Zicari is Co-Head of the Accounting and Management Control Department at ESSEC Business School, Director of the Management and Society track, and Academic Director of the Council on Business & Society. He is also the Honorary representative for Buenos Aires in Paris. He holds a PhD in Management Administration from the Universidad Nacional de Rosario, an MBA (Universidad Adolfo Ibáñez), and a BSc in Accounting. Adrián's career has spanned the corporate sector as Financial Manager and Controller and his academic research has been widely published in leading journals, among others, the *Journal of Business Ethics*, *Journal of Cleaner Production*, and *Social and Environmental Accountability Journal*.

Tom Gamble is Executive Director of the Council on Business & Society, running the operations, communications, and publications branches of the alliance. He holds an MA in Human Resource Management and Industrial Relations from Keele University as well as several coaching certifications. Tom's career has spanned teaching, lecturing, thought leadership, consulting, and instructional design, working with over 100 companies and educational institutions worldwide. He is a published author of fiction, non-fiction, and poetry.

Routledge CoBS Focus on Responsible Business
Series Editors: Tom Gamble and Adrián Zicari,
The Council on Business and Society (CoBS)

This series is published in collaboration with the Council on Business & Society (CoBS).

Routledge CoBS Focus on Responsible Business provides international and multicultural perspectives on responsible leadership and business practices in line with the UN SDGs. Contributors from leading business schools on five continents offer local, cultural, and global perspectives on the issues covered, drawing on high-level research and transforming it into engaging and digestible content for students, academics and practitioners.

Topics include but are not limited to: responsible finance and accounting, CSR and governance, supply chain management, leadership, diversity and inclusion, performance and innovation, responsible management, and well-being at work.

1. Responsible Finance and Accounting
Performance and Profit for Better Business, Society, and Planet
Edited by Adrián Zicari and Tom Gamble

2. Power and Corporate Responsibility
Dimensions, Purpose, and Value
Daniel Malan

3. The Employee and the Post-Pandemic Workplace
Towards a New, Enlightened Working Environment
Edited by Adrián Zicari and Tom Gamble

Created in 2011, The Council on Business & Society (CoBS) is an alliance of leading international business schools dedicated to educating today's and tomorrow's responsible leaders and managers. The member schools of the Council on Business & Society are convinced of the importance of business and management education in bringing research and culture for the economic and social development of their societies, countries, and the world. We are also convinced of the need for a multicultural approach to issues, practices, and projects, bringing both a global and local perspective on CSR and sustainability-related issues to learning, research and publications, and thought leadership for the wider public.

www.council-business-society.org

COUNCIL on
BUSINESS & SOCIETY
An alliance with a purpose

The Employee and the Post-Pandemic Workplace

Towards a New, Enlightened Working Environment

Edited by Adrián Zicari and Tom Gamble

Routledge
Taylor & Francis Group

LONDON AND NEW YORK

First published 2024
by Routledge
4 Park Square, Milton Park, Abingdon, Oxon OX14 4RN

and by Routledge
605 Third Avenue, New York, NY 10158

Routledge is an imprint of the Taylor & Francis Group, an informa business

British Library Cataloguing-in-Publication Data
A catalogue record for this book is available from the British Library

ISBN: 978-1-032-48362-7 (hbk)
ISBN: 978-1-032-48370-2 (pbk)
ISBN: 978-1-003-38868-5 (ebk)

DOI: 10.4324/9781003388685

Typeset in Times New Roman
by Deanta Global Publishing Services, Chennai, India

With kind acknowledgements to Pavan Jambai, Muskan Chourey, and Félix Dubois-Aubecq

Contents

Contributors

In order of appearance:

Adrián Zicari, ESSEC Business School (adrian.zicari@essec.edu)

Armand Bam, Stellenbosch Business School (armandb@usb.ac.za)

Michelle MacMahon, Trinity Business School, Trinity College Dublin (mmacmaho@tcd.ie)

Christine Zdelar, Trinity College Dublin (ZDELARC@tcd.ie)

Inigo Echeveste, ESSEC Business School (echeveste@essec.edu)

Mette Grangaard Lund, Technical Officer on Just transition and Green Jobs, International Labour Organization (ILO) (lundm@ilo.org)

Anca Metiu, ESSEC Business School (metiu@essec.edu)

Tanusree Jain, Copenhagen Business School (tja.msc@cbs.dk)

Louis Brennan, Trinity Business School, Trinity College Dublin (BRENNAML@tcd.ie)

Joana S.P. Story, FGV-EAESP (joana.story@fgv.br)

Filipa Castanheira, Nova School of Business and Economics (fcastanheira @novasbe.pt)

Beatriz Maria Braga, FGV-EAESP (Beatriz.Braga@fgv.br)

Germano Glufke Reis, School of Management Universidade Federal do Paraná (germanoglufkereis@yahoo.com.br)

Jordi Trullen, ESADE (jordi.trullen@esade.edu)

Veronica Casarin, ESSEC Business School (casarin@essec.edu)

Bernard Leca, ESSEC Business School (bernard.leca@essec.edu)

Stefan Linder, ESSEC Business School (linder@essec.edu)

Na Fu, Trinity Business School, Trinity College Dublin (FUNA@tcd.ie)

Peng He, School of Management Fudan University (hepeng@fudan.edu.cn)

Daniel Malan, Trinity Business School, Trinity College Dublin (daniel.malan@tcd.ie)

Ioana Lupu, ESSEC Business School (lupu@essec.edu)

Mayra Ruiz-Castro, University of Roehampton (Mayra.RuizCastro@roehampton.ac.uk)

Foreword

Armand Bam and Adrián Zicari

This second book in the 'Routledge and CoBS Focus on Responsible Business' series could not be more timely. Indeed, a focus on employees, their workplace and working conditions is an urgent need nowadays, as the global pandemic gradually leaves place for a new normal. But how will that 'new normal' be? Will it be really new? Will it be really normal? Conscious as we are that we find ourselves in the midst of a time of change, we can understandably be concerned about this issue. This ongoing change promises to shape the picture for employees during the coming years. Furthermore, this matters to us all, as a sizeable part of our lives is spent working, and most of us in firms and organisations.

While we are still all returning to 'normalcy', the shared experience of the global impact of COVID-19 is still to be realised. The research included in this book provides us with an opportunity to collect and connect with these experiences and insights. We are positive that through this approach we will assist leaders to develop not only a deeper understanding of the impact but also provide insights for practical application towards developing new, enlightened working environments. The shared learnings represent our contribution to a global effort to move businesses and societies forward. Moreover, it is in practice that we can achieve the excellence we desire, and we challenge those who read this book to reach beyond the confines of their geographical borders to understand and share new ways of committing to improving the work experiences of employees and leaders alike.

Our book, based on the collective research efforts of faculty from business schools on five continents, dares to be reasonably optimistic. With different research methods, with different data sources, coming from different geographies, all the studies mentioned in this book tend to support a project to significantly improve our working environments. Such a change is not only desirable; it is also feasible.

Digital tools allow us, even with significant time differences, to learn, exchange, and collaborate at a distance. But beyond technological tools, which were indeed available *before* the pandemic, the attitude of people has changed. We are now more open to meeting online, saving precious time and diminishing carbon emissions. We are now more open to working via collaborative platforms, increasing efficiency and speed. Granted, each technological solution brings its own set of new problems; as someone once said, *by inventing the car, car accidents were invented.* The same can be said of new social arrangements (e.g., the gig economy), which are not always exempt from controversy.

The pandemic has made us all acutely aware of the importance of work in the lives of citizens. Policies are important, but in the end, people lead people. It is the humanity and integrity with which we do this that is shaping our collective futures. The ability to construct and reconstruct working environments almost instantly has become a serious consideration for all those in leadership positions. And preparing for the unknown is now a daily consideration for all our businesses and institutions within society. Taking the time to reflect on this new challenge is an important task for all leaders and this book can act as a guide.

As it happens whenever the winds of change blow, new opportunities and risks arise. At the CoBS, as it is usually the case, we tend to look at the new opportunities, while not overlooking the impending new risks. We hope that this new book can help you, our dear reader, both in looking at the upcoming good and not overlooking the potential bad.

We do hope that you appreciate this new book.

1 The impact of the pandemic on employees and leaders

Christine Zdelar,
Michelle MacMahon, Armand Bam,
Adrián Zicari, Inigo Echeveste,
and Mette Grangaard Lund

Millennials

Lessons from COVID-19 lockdown and the future of work

Christine Zdelar and Michelle MacMahon

Monday. A Slack app huddle echoes from offices along the corridor. The hum of a team meeting going on in the room next door. A colleague pops their head in and asks for a quick update on a project. 10 am summons a group of friends to the break room for coffee and swapping stories from the weekend. You look up – and smile.

This is office life. Or how office life *once was* – five days a week. In early 2020, with the COVID-19 virus spreading to every continent, governments around the world decided to lockdown, forcing a previously unthinkable change in how people work. It meant an unprecedented shift – and shock – for both companies and employees.

Employees in particular were suddenly confronted with having to mentally and physically deal with this change: coping with fears and anxieties, the oddity of social distancing, and their organisations' crisis management measures. For the majority working from home, work and personal life suddenly merged, with virtual meetings and presentations bringing a whole new set of challenges in how to communicate with and be perceived by others. In the midst of this upheaval, Michelle MacMahon and Christine Zdelar decided to research how employees understood and coped with the disruption to their rites, habits, and approaches to work and performance.

Learning from Millennials

To explore how employees adapted to their new way of working, the researchers relied on something called *transactional distancing*, a framework previously developed for online education to understand the impact of distance learning on remote trainees – the psychological and intellectual effects, emotions, and indeed, the impact of distance on trainee performance.

DOI: 10.4324/9781003388685-2

Their method was to observe how workers made sense of this unexpected disruption in working habits through a sensemaking model developed by Wick (1995) in which a person traverses a process of dealing with an action, selecting relevant information from the event, and interpreting how to understand this in order to react to future events.

Of particular interest was to look at how the pandemic impacted Millennials, the generation born between the mid-1990s and the early 2000s and having grown up with the Internet. Indeed, this generation has little or no experience of the pre-Internet world.

The largest generational group in the USA, researchers have tended to find that Millennials prefer technology, virtual communication, and remote solutions over face-to-face interaction with others. Witness, for example, the rise of business models in recent years such as Uber Eats, virtual matchmaking or online chat groups and communities of friends. Given this, Millennials can provide more nuanced insights into the shift from face-to-face to remote distancing during the pandemic. Indeed, MacMahon and Zdelar chose to focus on Millennials as, for all else being equal, the reliance on technology to facilitate remote work would pose the least disruption to this group, making it possible to narrow in on the impact of transactional distance in this specific context.

The challenges of remote working

For teams and individuals to achieve goals within their organisations, they necessarily have to communicate and interact with others. They collaborate, brainstorm, negotiate, problem-solve, transfer ideas and knowledge to one another, and agree on processes to meet their objectives. Being distant from each other makes this all the more of a challenge.

This challenge stems from the reality that the transactional part of human interaction involves more than just words. Body language, gestures, touch, eye movement, facial expressions, mimicry, and tone of voice form a cocktail that helps assert our identity, social presence, and role. They also facilitate trust and understanding – or inversely, mistrust, and misunderstanding. Although these vectors of communication can appear on screen, the online effect – some might say *artificial environment* – reduces our confidence in accurately assessing these messages in real-time. In addition, technical or noise-pollution issues might also hamper things – jerky sound or video, for example, or the next-door neighbours deciding to knock down a wall in their kitchen while you're on a Team's call with the boss. All in all, the virtual poses challenges in our ability to exert control over how we present ourselves, the messages we wish to convey, and how we hope these messages will be understood by others.

It all makes sense

To return to the notion of sensemaking, when confronted by something unexpected or complex, we try to understand it and react with appropriate behaviours in order to deal with it. Stemming from research, sensemaking is defined as almost a creative process with people 'authoring' in order to build meaning from something complicated and even troubling. Weick states seven properties of sensemaking, three of which are particularly suited to analysing behaviours in times of crisis – socialization, enactment, and identity-building.

The former – *socialization* – is when an employee observes the behaviours of others to understand the problem and come up with options for how to respond. On the other hand, *enactment* applies to the employee's actions taken in an attempt to understand a problem or issue. Faced with a new situation, people will construct and take on an *identity* which they think is relevant to that situation and, as such, base their behaviour and decisions on who they believe themselves to be. For example, if someone witnesses a co-worker being unjustly reprimanded, they might take on the identity of a saviour – a white knight – and go to the rescue of their friend.

Behaviour: Adapt and adopt

MacMahon and Zdelar's research during lockdown showed that Millennials made use of these sensemaking factors in adapting and building new approaches to work. Because although tech savvy and displaying a preference for virtual interaction, the duration of imposed distancing – periods of lockdown sometimes stretching into several months in developed economies – coupled with going against the usual working norms confronted Millennials with something unique and difficult to adjust to.

Among the ten employees questioned, all of whom were working from home in the Washington, DC Metropolitan area, these sensemaking tactics enabled some to create greater efficiency. In effect, using sensemaking tactics, Millennials can self-regulate the potential negative impact of interacting at a distance.

Some employees might create a new, previously unexperienced identity and role – for example, a team member discovering that they have the knack for bringing people together in a virtual environment. Rather like a doctor and remote consultation, they might then take on the additional role of setting up regular check-ins to see how their colleagues are faring.

Others may enter the socialization and enactment dimensions of sensemaking – understanding the issue and adopting appropriate behaviour to deal with it – by adapting, for example, their way of communicating with their managers. One respondent stated this tactic, noting an improved and fuller response from her manager, which at the end of the day increased her overall performance and productivity and increased her ability to satisfy her manager's expectations.

A transformation: Positive though hard to go back to pre-2020

Working from home, then, gave rise to employees using three specific sensemaking dimensions during the pandemic and remote working: socialization, enactment, and identity building. These resulted in adopting different sets of behaviours from those they displayed pre-COVID-19 in the workplace. As such, Millennial employees developed a 'new normal.'

Mid-pandemic, MacMahon and Zdelar's research contended that this new mode and state of working, coupled with new behaviours, would pose a problem for companies post-pandemic in 're-educating' employees to return to their previous 'business as usual' ways of working. Indeed, the researchers envisaged organisations having to invest heavily in change management efforts to undo this 'new normal.' This seems to have been the case. Witness, for example, the UK with up to eight in ten employees surveyed by the Office for National Statistics stating that they wished to remain in remote working or at least continue to work in hybrid mode both at the office and at home. In some cases, there were even refusals to return to the office. In others, resignations.

Post-pandemic, firms and organisations have been obliged to re-think the workplace and employment packages to include well-being, extra-work leisure benefits, and pay increases. This indicates that lockdown and the remote working experience changed the Millennial employee's psychological contract with the organisation they work for.

As such, MacMahon and Zdelar's research during the pandemic raised a red flag for companies and organisations. Presuming that employees would return to re-opened offices and their old ways of working would be to underestimate the reality that Millennials had 'frozen' into their new normal. People had changed, and to un-change them back would require 'unfreezing' their new state.

For the employee post-COVID-19, however, the busy open spaces, ringing phones, chats with colleagues, coffee breaks, and after-work drinks might just not be the panacea that pre-pandemic society and their organisations thought necessary.

The 'New Normal' has indeed taken place. MacMahon and Zdelar believe the changes, including psychological, that Millennials adopted to working remotely during the pandemic have simply continued to the post-pandemic working norm in online meetings and hybrid working models. As a result, the pandemic provided the opportunity for employees to build new skills and their organisations a more flexible working arrangement. From an individual perspective, the new normal has become a preference for some who feel more productive, and for others who believe it is also more convenient regarding domestic obligations or long commutes.

The impact of the change on the wider perspective

According to MacMahon and Zdelar, the future can be viewed from at least four levels of analysis: commercial, organisational, team, and individual. At a commercial level, we can see changes in public transport that are less reliant on rail and bus. This is an advantage for the organisation when public transport workers go on strike as has been the case in the UK, with workers being able to simply pivot to working from home. On the other hand, it also means public transport workers are in a weaker position concerning their negotiations for higher pay.

Working from home has also had an impact on the retail and hospitality trade in the inner city with a shift to local neighbourhoods where many workers live and now also work. Moreover, working from home has had a knock-on effect on real estate with many companies – for example, State Street – reducing office space as employees now hot-desk.

At an organisational level, the 'new normal' has had an effect on corporate organisational structure, HR policies and practices, remote working technologies, and leadership style. Structure and strategy are aligned, to coin Cunningham and Harney. We can see an acceleration of a more fluid organisational structure – such as the organigraph – one that facilitates the flexibility of appropriate knowledge at appropriate times, and that facilitates workers choosing how and when to work.

The 'new normal' has whetted the appetite of employees towards job-crafting and HR are responding with strategies that support workers so that both parties find value in these working arrangements. However, these arrangements need to work in practice and, as such, organisations require remote working technologies that facilitate knowledge sharing and collaboration. These technologies extend to the home and local Wi-Fi capacity. Moreover, management and leaders need to be effective in leading individuals and teams when they may not get to meet in person as often, or ever, as they may have done in the past.

At an individual level, the new normal has had an effect on workers' skills. Skills that support their discipline to manage work-life balance, skills that support their communicating effectively online, and skills that facilitate their maintaining a healthy network of colleagues. As a result, an expected course of action would be for companies and organisations to change the type of training offered to employees.

Key takeaways

- The COVID-19 pandemic brought about unprecedented permanent change for both companies and employees
- Employees faced physical and mental challenges: fears, anxieties, social distancing, remote working, and virtual communication
- Using sensemaking, three dimensions – socialization, enactment, and identity-building – were found to apply to Millennials interviewed during the pandemic
- Socialization: An employee observes others to understand a problem and develops options to deal with it. Enactment: An employee's actions taken in an attempt to understand a problem or issue. Identity-building: An employee constructs a 'new identity' or role when faced with a new situation and which they think is relevant in how to deal with it
- During the pandemic, Millennial employees developed a 'new normal' of behaviour and working methods
- This has proven a major challenge for companies and organisations post-pandemic to make employees return to previous 'business as usual' behaviours and mindsets. Consequently, firms must resort to investing much time and effort in change management.

Food for thought

- Remember your own experience of the pandemic and remote working. How did you feel about it? What psychological challenges did you face and go through, and how did you cope with these?
- To what extent did you find interaction with your colleagues and team members hampered or facilitated by distance? By technology?
- Name three things that constituted the biggest change (break this down into positive and negative things) for you in terms of working methods and performance. How did you and your colleagues/team/company overcome them?

- What changes did you make to support your working from home? What changes have you maintained post-pandemic? And in what ways do these changes still support you?
- What changes did your organisation make to support your working from home? How has your company or organisation adapted to the post-pandemic? And in what ways do these changes still support you?

Related research: *How Millennials Made Sense of Transactional Distancing to Maintain Work Performance: A COVID-19 Investigation. OB Division Research Plenary: COVID-19 and Organizational Behavior, Annual Academy of Management Meeting, Virtual, August 2020. Conference Paper. Christine Zdelar and Michelle MacMahon, Trinity Business School, Trinity College Dublin.*

References

Brown, A. D., Stacey, P. K. and Nandhakumar, J. (2008). Making Sense of Sensemaking Narratives. Human Relations, Vol. 61, p. 1035, Available at SSRN: https://ssrn.com/abstract=1632910

Shotter, J. (1993). Becoming Someone: Identity and Belonging. In N. Coupland and J. F. Nussbaum (Eds.), Discourse and Lifespan Identity (pp. 5–27). Sage Publications, Inc.

Weick, K. E. (1995). Sensemaking in Organizations, Volume 3. Sage Publications, Inc.

Mintzberg, H. and Van der Heyden, L. (1999). Organigraphs: Drawing How Companies Really Work. Harvard Business Review, Vol. 77(5), pp. 87–94, 184.

COVID-19 and the impact on women

An insight on academia in South Africa

Armand Bam

A time when women academics' emotional well-being was on a knife edge

While the COVID-19 pandemic occurred progressively, and yet so abruptly, in most countries, not only physical health was jeopardized. In a situation that was initially completely unthinkable at the outbreak of the pandemic, a majority of countries decided to implement social restrictions and lockdown measures. For some people, these regulations led to acute and post-acute neuropsychiatric sequelae, including increased fatigue, cognitive impairments, anxiety, and depressive symptoms. Nonetheless, it is not entirely clear, or at least not entirely measurable, that the pandemic increased psychological disorders. It is more accurate to outline that the psychological responses to COVID-19 and the measures taken as a result were heterogeneous according to population sub-groups.

Among the population, women were one of the most vulnerable sub-groups, tending to report a greater increase in psychological disorders than men in response to the COVID-19 pandemic. Research has pointed to the cause of this stress as being the increase in their workload, facilitated by the move to e-learning, as one of the first sources of emotional taxation. Other studies also outlined that the increase in job insecurity during the pandemic was greater than the loss of productivity and the increase in workload during this period. In the academic field, this effect was inevitably reinforced among instructors holding short-term contracts or contractual work agreements.

Parenthood was also one of the most differentiating factors between men and women during the pandemic, with women, particularly those with children, impacted most. The balance between parental and professional

DOI: 10.4324/9781003388685-3

life was especially strained during this period, given the measures to close schools and childcare services.

A matter of '*emotional taxation*'

This combination of factors may have led to a source of deep emotional disorders for some university women, which the study by Ronnie, Bam, and Walters highlights through the lens of '*emotional taxation*.' Three major factors contributed to the development of emotional taxation among women academics.

Work environment

The primary source of emotional taxation reported by the study was the work environment, with 94% of the academics who reported experiences of emotional taxation acknowledging having experienced this source of stress.

This may be attributed to the fact that academics had to deal with the emotional burden on students, the inadequacy of students' digital tools to cope with distance work, and the need to provide ongoing support to students in the context of e-learning. For their part, academics found themselves in a situation of inadequacy regarding technical equipment and work in the context of the transition to home offices, as well as a lack of planning on the part of their universities. The need to juggle their family and professional lives became much more acute in this context, with the burden of their work itself becoming more oppressive.

While all academics faced these difficulties, they were particularly severe for women academics. Moreover, female faculty members tended to be more heavily involved in supporting students. Lacking training and experience in this area, support became time-consuming and emotionally draining, leading some female instructors to experience burnout.

An unbalanced home life

The second factor inducing the appearance of emotional taxation among academic women was linked to a home life problem. Bam et al.'s research identified that 55% of the women academics who reported emotional taxation issues recognised this factor as a cause.

More precisely, the research reports a general feeling of increased family burdens while family support structures were unavailable. At the height of the social restraint and containment measures, schools were closed and support circles, such as friends, family, and professionals, were cut off. The burden of family responsibilities tended to fall more on women, with one female academic notably mentioning that the job of dealing with household chores, ensuring food and cooking for the family, and looking after the health and welfare matters for a number of loved ones had, in general, become the heavy burden of women to mainly bear.

This burden was exacerbated in the case of single women with children, who then had no support or opportunity to look after themselves due to lack of time. In addition to family responsibilities, the confinement of single women, especially when they had just entered the profession and/or arrived in a new town became an issue of concern. Not surprisingly, a feeling of social isolation quickly took over as a result.

But while this sense of social isolation was less marked in traditional family patterns, women nonetheless experienced the need to prioritise the needs of their family members over their own needs.

When the social milieu and women academics' well-being intertwine

39% of the women reporting experiences of emotional taxation also acknowledged a third source of emotional disorder: their social milieu. This refers to the pressure of social relationships that may have been exerted during this period: either supporting loved ones, dealing with their expectations, and/or managing loss for those whose loved ones had died during the pandemic. Indeed, COVID-19 could be said to have added to the stress of lost income, increased family burdens, and anxiety. Moreover, women academics reported situations where they spent a significant amount of time mentally supporting loved ones who were unable to cope with anxiety themselves. Some also took responsibility for ensuring that the elderly people around them were safe. However, these actions also led to negative psychological consequences and a loss of time to deal with other priorities.

As such, a variety of coping strategies were used by women academics, including reprioritisation, self-talk, and faith. On the flip side, these strategies may have led to a depreciation of their academic work and failed to prevent a general feeling of frustration and emotional exhaustion.

Has work–life balance vanished into thin air?

Finally, given the experiences of emotional taxation among women academics, some pointed to the cause as being a '*work–life merge.*' In other words, as the confinement imposed in South Africa led to female academics working from home, their personal space also became an office and a classroom.

This impact of the pandemic, added to social restraint measures, has not been without effect on female academics. While Bam et al.'s research reports that some women took the opportunity to reconnect with their children, others found themselves in an inextricable situation of stress. The imbalance of household and family tasks within couples exacerbated the problem. In addition, the 'work–life merge' prevented them from bonding with colleagues and increased the isolation of some people, especially those living alone.

In response to these problems, several female academics in the research explained that they had decided to distance themselves from their roles and – stepping out to the balcony, as it were – reduce their workloads to concentrate more on activities that would help them maintain their mental health. However, this reduction in workload may have been accompanied by a reduction in their research and less urgent, though important, work tasks.

Ronnie, Bam, and Walters' research concludes that there is an accordion effect on female academics – events happening during the pandemic accumulating physical and psychological effects that may occur further down the line into the post-pandemic. The 'work–life merge' has led some of them to manage family and professional tasks and emotional pressure simultaneously, leading to significant levels of stress and anxiety. Beyond the emotional aspect, this situation has had a negative impact on their academic performance, leading ultimately to delays in research and a reduction in the volume of research papers produced – something that highlights an inequality with their male academics who managed to come through the pandemic with fewer scars.

Key takeaways

- The COVID-19 pandemic did not exactly lead to an increase in psychological sequelae but was more accurately characterized by a number of various effects and responses to the pandemic. Among the population, the well-being of women academics was particularly jeopardized
- A study conducted on 2,029 women academics in South Africa concluded that nearly 17% of its respondents experienced '*emotional taxation*' during the confinement period in South Africa
- Three major sources of emotional taxation were identified: the work environment; an unbalanced home life, and the pressure from the social milieu
- These experiences of emotional taxation were above all the consequence of the '*work–life merge*,' made all the more possible when confined, where the office and the classroom blended with women academics' home life
- The greater vulnerability of female academics to emotional taxation during the COVID-19 pandemic in South Africa also reveals gender

inequality, not only in terms of psychological distress but also in terms of career.

Food for thought

- If you are a student, and you lived through the pandemic and remote classes, how did your teacher or professor cope? To what extent did you see any signs of additional stress and fatigue?
- What was your attitude during the pandemic and/or lockdown? How did your behaviours and habits change and what impact did distance learning have on your ability to study and obtain good grades?
- Imagine you are part of a government think tank. What measures would you propose to cater for women at work during a possible future pandemic/lockdown situation? How could employers help, especially in terms of providing support for women with children?
- What measures would you take to make the population aware of gender inequality in your country?

Related research: *Emotional Wellbeing: The Impact of the COVID-19 Pandemic on Women Academics in South Africa. Linda Ronnie, Armand Bam, and Cyrill Walters, Frontiers in Education, 10.3389/feduc.2022.770447.*

Reference

How COVID-19 shaped mental health: from infection to pandemic effects, B. Penninx et al., *Nature Medicine*, 2022.

There is no New Normal

Welcome to the new Schumpeterian world

Inigo Echeveste and Adrián Zicari

Towards the end of the COVID-19 crisis which saw the pandemic stabilizing in major markets, there was an ongoing discussion about how the world after the crisis would be. Whether the New Normal would imply more or fewer changes in our world. Whether home working would become the new standard for working or not. And whether widespread digital technologies, major investments in infrastructure, and changes in patterns of consumption would bring fundamental change in our economy or not.

Still a matter of reflection, the danger for corporate leaders is to conceive the next scenario, whatever it happens to be, as the New Normal. That is, a new situation of stability after a crisis, a macro context that would carry on for a significant horizon. We consider instead that the next scenario, whatever it is, will not last for long. We consider instead that we are entering into a succession of unstable scenarios, amid episodes of rapid change and disruption. Welcome to the new Schumpeterian world.

The paradox of stable instability

As academics, we have been studying these issues for some years while engaging in conversations with business leaders in executive education and in consulting activities. This experience supports our conviction that we are entering a time of political, social, and economic *stable instability*. Change will be the only constant. One can no longer make decisions with a framework developed for another era. Our mindset has to evolve.

In times of the 'old normal' – at least for the major industrial economies – the implicit notion concerning the economic environment entailed long periods of stability, moderate growth, and low or no inflation. While a crisis in one or another industrial sector could eventually arise, and some companies could occasionally run into trouble, the big picture was that of stability for the long run. In that stable context, competition would drive profits down to the higher satisfaction of clients. Companies could be profitable

DOI: 10.4324/9781003388685-4

in the long run only by shielding themselves from market competition. *Avoiding competition* was the only path to sustainable profits.

In that vein, Porter posited that companies should carve out a place in the market by choosing an advantageous position vis-à-vis suppliers, clients, substitutes, and new entrants. The ideal situation was having a few companies competing among themselves in a precise, well-determined segment of the market. In such a stable world, the strategy was about choosing, looking for a particular place in the market, and deciding what to do and perhaps more importantly, what not to do. Once business leaders had made a good strategic choice for their companies, the rest was mainly an optimisation of resources, good HR practices, prudent finances, efficient supply chains, and the like. That is sound management, as it is still taught in the best business schools today.

Not so much an Industrial Revolution as a *Knowledge Revolution*

This is no longer the case. The notion of VUCA (Volatility, Uncertainty, Complexity, Ambiguity) is not new. But to this day, its use has been mostly limited to the community of strategists, both in the military and in academia, and frequently reserved for exceptional contexts (i.e., a war or an economic crisis). Now we are seeing an expansion of the VUCA environment both in scale (global) and in time (permanent).

However, it would be tempting to simply attribute this expansion to the COVID-19 crisis. Granted, the pandemic was an unexpected (while not *unexpectable*) situation, with major consequences all over the world and with unclear outcomes. However, we contend that the COVID-19 crisis did not create this VUCA context. Important as the COVID-19 crisis was, *it is a mere catalyser of a global, ongoing revolution*, whose seeds were planted much before with the development and dissemination of digital tools.

To be sure, digital tools have been there for years. But the COVID-19 crisis has been the occasion, the stepping point, where society massively appropriates that technology. Making a parallel with Christensen's disruption model, the disruptive trajectory of digital technology accelerated during the COVID-19 crisis, thus challenging incumbent business practices all over the world.

Put differently, this is not a new step in the Industrial Revolution (either 3.0, 4.0, or any figure). This is indeed a *Knowledge Revolution*, where knowledge (and its application, now unleashed by the global spread of digital tools) is the driver of profitability. These technologies, bringing more flexibility and fewer constraints, now allow companies to redesign their industrial processes from scratch, thus doing *tabula rasa* of incumbent business models. Employees are no longer paid for their attendance at the office, but for their knowledge and skills, increasingly deployed from anywhere. We are witnessing a tremendous change in consumption patterns and lifestyle choices and preferences. Some industrial sectors strive, whereas others struggle.

Welcome to the new Schumpeterian world

In this stable instability, merely finding and securing a strong competitive position in a market is no longer a guarantee of success. Furthermore, with the exception of strongly regulated markets, most markets are becoming porous, their boundaries being no longer as clear as they were before. And this trend is continuing after decades of deregulation in major economies.

Welcome to the new Schumpeterian world. Creative destruction, the expression that Joseph Schumpeter coined in the mid-twentieth century, is an ambivalent concept. On one hand, there is of course destruction of markets and companies and asset impairment. This can be sad, unsettling, and worrying. But on the other hand, and perhaps most interestingly, it brings the creation of new markets and new opportunities to seize. In this context, corporate leaders – nay *intrapreneurs* – have to look beyond the supposed boundaries of their markets. In 'Schumpeterland,' value is no longer created by savvy positioning plus efficient resource optimisation and cost control kept over time. Value is increasingly achieved by finding opportunities in the midst of ever-changing markets, focusing on evolving client needs, and harnessing the power of digital information for that purpose.

In this new world, corporate strategy is no longer a top-down exercise. Frequent, surprising change makes conventional strategising increasingly difficult. Five-year plans become obsolete before the ink is dry. Strategic plans cannot be changed overnight or several times in the same year. Opportunities appear anywhere. Corporations can no longer afford the luxury of time. One cannot wait for the next board meeting.

As Andy Grove used to say, only the paranoid survive. Instead of becoming paranoid, we propose some insights for preparing ourselves to develop emerging strategies, much in line with Mintzberg. Companies should develop and nurture a learning culture that prepares itself for unexpected changes that can arise at any moment. This concept is far from new. When Napoleon invaded Spain in the early nineteenth century, the structured, well-organised Imperial Army was challenged and eventually lost to the local guerrillas (incidentally, *guerrilla* means 'small war' in Spanish). Despite their obvious limitations in terms of armament, these agile, highly dynamic, and persistent guerrillas won over the most powerful army in Europe.

Unconventional planning for an unconventional fight

Drawing from this inspiration, that is, guerrilla warfare instead of a conventional battle, we propose some insights for these interesting times:

- Do not plan, learn. There is no point in drafting elaborate mission statements, visions, and the like. Granted, short-time planning would always be useful in terms of resource coordination, particularly in production and finance. We continue teaching budgeting in our Exec Ed sessions. But the corporate focus has to be on corporate learning and finding new market opportunities. Think of Amazon Web Services, initially a side activity, which is now a major source of profit for that company
- Develop a learning culture, not a cost-cutting culture. While sometimes cost-cutting can be a necessity, cost-cutting in itself is not a strategy. There is no value creation, merely a reduction of excessive costs. Corporate leaders instead need to nurture a culture of corporate learning, allowing companies to rapidly adapt to clients' expectations. Furthermore, we claim that in this VUCA context, a corporate culture adapted to this environment is indeed a strategy
- Learn as a company, not as an individual. Knowledge from individuals is of course important. However, the best companies try and achieve to learn as organisations, and this learning remains in the company even when individuals leave the firm. In particular, Design Thinking methodologies should be used not only for product creation but moreover as a mindset for major decisions. This is the case with Airbnb, where two of their co-founders are designers by training
- Do not hire people on their credentials only. Look also for adaptable skills, which could be deployed in contexts we do not imagine now. We should hire people not for their aptitude but for their attitude. Seniority is no longer key, learning speed is. Moreover, these attitudes are not the monopoly of the young. Curiosity and openness to innovation are the talents of today's workforce.

Sooner or later, the COVID-19 crisis will completely end. What will not end, but will indeed accelerate, is the *Knowledge Revolution*. Corporate leaders should take note of this epochal change, and refrain from any expectation of aiming for a New Normal (or worse, coming back to business as usual). Company readiness is the key to survival in these Schumpeterian times.

Key takeaways

- The pandemic is over and the danger for corporate leaders is to conceive the next scenario as the New Normal – a new situation of stability after a crisis. However, the authors consider the world is entering into a succession of unstable scenarios, amid episodes of rapid change and disruption

- It is a time of political, social, and economic *stable instability*. Now we are seeing an expansion of the VUCA (Volatility, Uncertainty, Complexity, Ambiguity) environment both in scale (global) and in time (permanent)
- The COVID-19 crisis is a mere catalyser of a global, ongoing revolution, whose seeds were planted much before with the development and dissemination of digital tools
- A *Knowledge Revolution* is underway spurred by digital technologies
- In this stable instability, finding and securing a strong competitive position in a market is no longer a guarantee of success. Corporate leaders, with an intrapreneurs mindset, have to look beyond the supposed boundaries of their markets
- Value is increasingly achieved by finding opportunities in the midst of ever-changing markets, focusing on evolving client needs, and harnessing the power of digital information for that purpose
- Companies should develop and nurture a learning culture that prepares them for unexpected changes that can arise at any moment
- Recommendations for this stable instability for companies are: Do not plan, learn; develop a learning culture, not a cost-cutting culture; learn as a company, not only as an individual; and do not hire people on their credentials only. Look also for adaptable skills, which could be deployed in contexts we do not imagine now.

Food for thought

- How has your professional environment changed post-pandemic? To what extent has your organisation returned to the same ways as before? Or has it changed? How?
- Looking back over the last ten years, to what extent do you agree with the authors that instability is a constant? What has happened on a local, national, and international level to support your conclusion? How comfortable do you feel about this?
- Project yourself into the next ten years. What do you see happening in your company or organisation? What world events are probable that may shape or disrupt things? And what new skills do you think you will have to learn in order to successfully navigate the decade ahead?

Why climate change can determine your future job and what to do about it

Mette Grangaard Lund

It was not much more than a year ago that I, for the first time, realized that the beautiful yellow rapeseed fields, the green meadows, and the pine tree forests I knew from my childhood in Denmark were not just nature. Rather they are industry, agriculture, farming, and forestry – they are jobs. Worldwide more than 1.2 billion jobs, or 40 percent of total employment,[1] rely on so-called ecosystem services (such as air and water purification, soil renewal, timber, natural gas, and pollination, to mention a few[2]). Despite the clear link between the World of Work and nature, the jobs and people aspect of climate change continues to be an overlooked dimension in policy, business strategy, and among workers.

Today, most people around the world can feel how climate change impacts their daily lives with spikes in food prices, homes becoming prone to natural disasters and more expensive to insure,[3] the pollution of air, water, and food, or supply chains getting disrupted. In fact, global warming may be the biggest health threat facing humanity, according to the World Health Organization.[4]

Meanwhile, climate and environmental change are becoming increasingly important to businesses and the private sector. The World Economic Forum's Global Risk Report from 2023[5] shows how five of the most impactful short-term risks for businesses are linked to environment and climate change. Perhaps more surprisingly, an additional three out of ten business risks were linked to social disruptions. Given that the two dimensions depend so much on each other for stability, one could argue that it would be insufficient for companies (or governments) to address them separately. Simply put, merging ambitious climate action with social justice is called 'a just transition.'[6]

DOI: 10.4324/9781003388685-5

Is the concept of a just transition the missing link between the E, S, and G?

As sustainability concepts made their inroads into academia and businesses, they were eventually linked to the concepts of the triple bottom line or the three P's of people, planet, and profit,[7] the UN Sustainable Development Goals (SDGs) and Environmental, Social, Governance (ESG) standards, frameworks, and rankings.[8] Despite environmental and climate progress in some areas, the social deficit in businesses continues to make headlines worldwide, ranging from modern-day slavery; to people losing their livelihoods to floods or drought; to workers being made redundant as companies and societies transition towards carbon neutrality. Clearly, the 'S' or 'people' dimension has been the blind spot for businesses and governments in their environmental sustainability strategies. According to the International Labour Organization (ILO), a just transition towards environment sustainability must be based on effective social dialogue among all groups impacted and respect for fundamental labour principles and rights. In other words, it couples ambitious climate action (E) with decent work (S), as well as offers a process and way forward (G). Unfortunately, a just transition will not come by itself.

How does climate change impact the labour market?

First, from a labour perspective we must fear climate *in*-action rather than the transition itself. For example, some scenarios suggest that unmitigated climate change could push 100 million people into poverty by 2030.[9] On the other hand, yet quite fittingly, ILO data shows that if managed well, the transition to renewable energy and circularity could lead to 100 million jobs created by 2030.[10]

From a business perspective, the greening of businesses is linked to cost reduction and higher productivity, access to finance, new markets, and lower input costs, among others. Along the same line, in-action will negatively impact companies as heat stress leads to loss of work hours,[11] and natural disasters increase the cost of capital (amongst a few business case examples).[12] The impact will differ between countries, regions, and industries, but in the bigger picture, companies, as well as employees and job seekers, stand to win from a just transition.

What does a job look like in an environmentally sustainable economy?

When you imagine a green job in the future, perhaps you envision workers in hard hats raising windmills, or a well-dressed sustainability manager

with solid carbon budget calculations. Predicting the future is always difficult, but economic modelling can give us some scenarios for labour market
changes. The reality is that, recently, and particularly due to COVID-19,
working conditions and wages have worsened, and informality is yet on the
rise globally.[13] Because sustainable economic development must consider
the social dimension of change, progress must support the 'decent work'[14]
agenda. Reverting to environmental and climate change, it is necessary to
ask whether jobs and industries that produce negative externalities (such as
climate change, biodiversity loss, or pollution) and affect other workers can
be considered decent jobs. Therefore, the ILO is persisting that green jobs
must be decent jobs to ensure that economies and societies develop in a way
that leaves no one behind.

However, with the right government policies, enabling environment, and
company policies, all jobs can be green jobs in the future. In fact, according
to the ILO, green jobs are all decent jobs that:

A. Contribute to preserving or restoring the environment (across all sectors, not only agriculture or renewable energy)
B. Produce goods or provide services that benefit the environment (such
   as climate-neutral housing construction or clean transportation) despite
   not always being green in the production process
C. Contribute to more environmentally friendly processes (such as supply chain management or circularity initiatives) but do not necessarily
   produce environmental goods or services.

In other words, you can distinguish between jobs in green economic sectors
from an output and a process perspective. Suddenly, you might see that your
job prospects look much greener. Still, the types of jobs we will need in the
future may not be so different from the ones we have today, but the skills-
sets for green jobs will be very important.

Knowledge is power

Lastly, the main changes in the labour markets will not be job creation or
job loss but rather how jobs change and how we will deal with this change.
In some countries and industries, the change will be massive. For example,
the circular economy scenario indicates that 78 million jobs can be created
in shifting to circularity, while 71 million jobs will be lost. The green transition could potentially be a labour market change on a scale of that of the
Industrial Revolution but would take place over a few decades rather than
a century. ILO data shows how some jobs will be in higher demand (such
as sales and trades workers), whereas others will become redundant (such

as labourers in mining and some types of construction, manufacturing, and transport workers). Yet, any job gains are conditional on investments in training to avoid skills mismatches.

So, what skills will you need to make your career to be as smooth as possible through the transition? Of course, it depends on your education and occupational background. But, you may be surprised to see that the examples of skills that overlap in growing and declining industries include easily transferable 'core' skills such as organizational skills, English, computer literacy, scheduling, forklift operation, sales, and marketing.[15] In conclusion, policymakers must anticipate the skills needs for the transition, and educators and training institutions must collaborate closely with employers and workers to close the skills gaps for facilitating green labour market mobility. Similarly, learners and workers must better understand how their existing skill sets can be redeployed in other jobs and industries throughout their careers.

The great green reshuffle

Reflecting on the climate challenge and labour market changes ahead of us leaves us with the question, how will we manage? Climate change will impact people and businesses differently, depending on several things including geography, demography, gender, and industry. This is important to keep in mind when we think about how to cope and adapt because no one size fits all. For the sake of this short piece, let us consider the case of the European Union.

Generally, labour markets tend to react to economic changes with a slight lag,[16] yet we have seen swift corrections in times of crisis. A telling example is the response to the most recent labour market shock caused by COVID-19, where governments, workers, and employers quickly had to adapt to dampen the blow on employment. Post-pandemic, we are seeing new trends towards workers in certain regions and occupations that either quit their jobs or change their way of working completely. Terms such as 'the great resignation,' 'great reshuffle,' or 'great rethink' have been coined by consultancies and journalists, which all have in common that power and agency are being moved towards employees as workers become more aware of what they demand from working life.

However, the greatest reshuffle may be yet to come as economies and societies will have to transition to mitigate and adapt to climate change. It leaves us with the question of whether we can expect further agency shifted towards employees as workers search for decent work that is also green. Perhaps, in the near future, you will be on your way home from work, look out the bus window at the water, soil, and air gliding by, and quietly thank nature for yet another great day of work.

Key takeaways

- Decent work is a part of Sustainable Develop Goal 8 and is both a key driver for and a result of climate action. It is hard to imagine a net-zero future where jobs, economies, and societies do not all work towards decarbonization and sustainability. Likewise, it is hard to imagine a sustainable future without focusing on decent work
- ILO Labour market data and modelling suggest that keeping global warming below 2 degrees will create 100 million new jobs by 2030. However, 80 million jobs may also be redundant in the process
- Rather than focusing on the jobs created or lost, the major labour market change will be in those millions of jobs that will be transformed or substituted. Greening the labour market will be a large transformation economy wide
- The skill sets in demand in, for example, a renewable energy or circular economy scenario are, in particular core skills that, with the right skills and employment strategies, could be easily transferable from existing jobs
- Green jobs will be created across all skill levels, but particularly amongst medium- and highly-skilled professions. Ensuring that schools and universities equip their students with the skills needed for these green jobs is essential – both for students' employability and the scale and speed of the transition to environmental, climate, and economic sustainability

Food for thought

- Worldwide 1.2 billion jobs depend directly on ecosystem services (such as air, water, pollination etc.). What kind of ecosystem services does your job depend on?
- Sustainability and work quality are becoming increasingly important for employees when considering their next job. What qualities matter to you in a future job (e.g. working conditions such as flexible working hours, salary, security, or perhaps employee involvement and rights)?
- What does a green job look like to you? Where does the person work – in an office or a construction site? What conditions do they work under? What kind of skills do you think the person needs to stay relevant in a green economy?
- Not all jobs that may benefit the environment are decent jobs. Can you think of some jobs that might benefit the environment but do not align with the SDG goal of decent work?

Notes

1 World Employment and Social Outlook (2018) *Greening with Jobs* (ilo.org).
2 MEA (Millennium Ecosystem Assessment) (2005) *Ecosystems and Human Well-Being: Synthesis.*
3 See for example Moody's 2021 risk report of how climate change impacts companies risk exposure across sectors. All evaluated sectors have more than 40% of their facilities highly exposed to risks such as physical flooding/heat, hurricane, water or wildfire.
4 Climate Change and Health (who.int).
5 *Global Risks Report* (2023) World Economic Forum (weforum.org).
6 A Just Transition means greening the economy in a way that is as fair and inclusive as possible to everyone concerned, creating decent work opportunities and leaving no one behind. See more useful information on the ILO website.
7 A concept popularised by John Elkington in the mid 90s, and quickly adopted by academics, professionals, and policy makers. From a notion of sustainable development, 'prosperity' rather than profit, may be a more suitable term.
8 GRI has made an easy overview and example of the many types of standards, frameworks, and rankings that could fit under the ESG-umbrella.
9 Hallegatte et al. (2016) *Shockwaves: Managing the Impacts of Climate Change on Poverty* (Washington, DC: World Bank).
10 The Paris Agreement is a legally binding international treaty on climate change from 2015, where 196 parties to the UN Climate Change Conference (more csommonly known as COP) agreed to hold 'the increase in the global average temperature to well below 2°C above pre-industrial levels.' The Paris agreement and temperature target continue to be the aim for global climate action. For more information go to UNFCCC.
11 ILO (2019) *Working on a Warmer Planet.*
12 See for example ILO (2022) *Greening Enterprises: Transforming Processes and Workplaces for More Business Case Arguments and Examples.*
13 ILO (2023) *World Employment and Social Outlook Trends 2023.*
14 Decent work refers to the quality of the job, and has four key components, job creation, social security, rights at the workplace, and social dialogue. To better understand what makes up a decent job, the ILO decent work indicators may be interesting to look at.
15 For more examples of core and technical skills in a circular and renewable energy scenario see the report by ILO (2019) Skills for a Greener Future.
16 ILO (2022) *ILO Monitor on the World of Work.* Tenth edition.

Microcase

You are the CEO of a medium-sized subsidiary of a large marketing agency with offices around the country and overseas branches in Singapore and the USA.

During the pandemic, and in line with government recommendations, your company resorted to remote working arrangements for all employees. While initially tough, your teams quickly managed to get to grips with the new ways of working, overcoming challenges, and soon returning to their usual high performance. After several months of lockdown, large-scale vaccination of the workforce, and the gradual decrease in the number of infections and gravity of the cases, the government announced that things could return to normal and employees go back to their former working ways.

That was several months ago now. And your company still faces several serious issues. First, many employees actually prefer to continue with remote working; at first disregarding calls from HR to return to the office, and then only coming back begrudgingly. HR has informed you that since the return to normal office hours, absenteeism has increased by a hefty 20%. Moreover, analyzing the phenomenon, you realise that although many of the cases stem from tiredness and depression-related causes, there are clear indications that some cases are linked to a lack of employee motivation to change their remote working habits.

In addition, staff turnover has increased over the last three months to reach an alarming 25%. This is bad news for the company, as losing talent and acquiring new staff causes costs to the company to skyrocket and performance levels to plummet. What's more, the job market has become very tight in general since the end of restrictions, with studies pointing to employees having used the period of the pandemic to question what is essential to them.

You are faced with a dilemma. So far, you have remained adamant on the fact that all employees return to the office as per pre-COVID-19. If you continue this, you are aware that motivation will drop further, and the

DOI: 10.4324/9781003388685-6

leaving rate will only increase. In the end run, performance and quality will drop with an obvious knock-on effect on client satisfaction and perhaps even retention.

- What do you intend to do? Give way to employee representative pressure and offer a full return to remote working?
- Offer a halfway, hybrid measure? And if so, what sort of arrangements?
- How can you stem the outward flow of employees but at the same time ensure that both discipline is safeguarded and the office infrastructure you had invested in pre-pandemic is used?
- How can you ensure team spirit, interaction, and morale?
- In your experience, what happened after the end of lockdown? How fast or how slow did it take to come back to normalcy?
- How is this new 'normalcy?' Exactly the same (business as usual), or with some adaptations, changes, or improvements?
- And you, how did the lockdown change you in terms of new skills, attitude, and new expectations?

2 Managing and adapting to remote and hybrid working

Anca Metiu, Tanusree Jain,
and Louis Brennan

Out of sight, but not out of mind

Anca Metiu

While social psychology principles suggest that individuals living closer to each other are more likely to form relationships as compared to those who are further away, researchers have begun to question its validity in today's world of intertwined social networks. The rapid inclusion of video conferencing and instant messaging in our lives has disrupted notions of both personal as well as professional communication. For instance, traditionally, co-workers who have desks close to each other would often bump into each other, engage in conversations about their lives outside the workplace, and eventually strike up a friendship.

In the post-pandemic era, teleworking has left minimum room for the good ol' water cooler chats. Some employers are worried this might harm professional relationship dynamics and employee productivity and are hoping to resume in-office work. But is bringing employees together in the same physical space the only way to overcome disconnection?

Contradictory to our conventional wisdom, geographically distant co-workers sometimes feel even closer to each other than colleagues in the same office. This behaviour does not align with the objective definition of proximity. Looking at it subjectively, we obtain a construct of 'perceived proximity,' which reflects an individual's perception of how close or far another individual is. Looking at this construct in detail can help us take a step back and reassess the importance given to physical proximity and achieve the benefits of colocation without having employees work in the same office.

Miles apart, close at heart

Physical proximity influences connections among colleagues to a certain extent but several other dimensions often go unnoticed and are equally, if not more, important to develop bonds between employees. The forced shift to remote work in recent times made it easier to analyse these dimensions

DOI: 10.4324/9781003388685-8

independent of the geographical distance because it didn't matter if your team member used to work in the office next to yours or was based miles away; you still had to connect with them virtually due to the lockdown and current working conditions.

In this situation, since distance becomes irrelevant and the mode of communication is the same, the frequency, interactivity, and depth of the conversation would impact your perception of how close you are to a colleague. Take an example from your everyday life – you would probably not mind walking a couple of blocks more to get your coffee from the lady who regularly greets you and remembers your order instead of a shop that is closer to your home but does not offer similar service when you go there. In a professional context too it is observed that communicating frequently about the project's progress and engaging in comprehensive conversations about the goals with team members leads to a sense of collectiveness.

Having a common ground

It can sometimes be easier to maintain relations despite the distance if you believe that you share some characteristics or experiences with the other person. People regularly tend to discover and create common identities with others either at their workplace or at a distance. Once the state of identification – through common interests, culture, experiences, and job expertise, for example – and an impression of inclusion is achieved in a peer group, it becomes easier to understand and become closer to each other because the sense of identification leads to positive attributions in absence of real data.

For instance, consider the situation where you are experiencing a delayed response from your colleague about the completion of his tasks. There are two possible reactions to this. First, being critical of your co-worker, and questioning his competency and work ethic. Second, coming from a space of concern and care, offering them support because you know he recently moved to a new city, and you understand how overwhelming it can become as an ex-pat yourself.

Finding the sweet spot

Communication and identification in a group are both interrelated to some extent and contribute to feelings of mutual understanding. The process of communicating helps people discover the social values they share with others and gradually make them feel closer.

Nevertheless, 'perceived proximity' is a complex construct, and it is premature to conclude that communicating more would always lead to better relationships. In some cases, when individuals communicate with each other too often and/or about superficial and irrelevant topics, instead of feeling connected and close, feelings of hostility and annoyance start to arise.

Socio-organizational factors affecting perceived proximity

So far, we have been revitalizing the concepts of proximity in this insight by discussing how being geographically close to someone and feeling close and connected to someone are different things. Now, to understand how an organization can apply this knowledge of 'perceived proximity' to improve the virtual working environment, let's dig deeper into the factors affecting communication and identification.

A closely-knit organizational network with stronger norms is conducive to improved and effective communication. It also allows the members to easily maintain relations which is even more crucial in virtual teams. Additionally, when the organization offers structural assurance to its employees in the form of safeguards, such as legal recourse and technological features, employees communicate freely. Consequently, they feel comfortable in being their true self which opens the possibility of creating a shared identity even with members at a distance.

Technology plays a key role in both building a stronger network structure and facilitating structural assurance. We are already aware of how telecommunication tools bring us closer to one another. Another benefit of technologies such as open-source infrastructure is that it makes collaboration easier and more transparent.

Remote is here to stay – and so is perceived proximity

Since remote work is here to stay, it is great news for employers and managers that being geographically distant can co-exist with having the feeling of being close. There are several ways in which organizations increase the perceptions of proximity in their members and bring them closer without resorting to face-to-face interaction.

Managing distance between team members demands significant costs and resources. However, thoughtfully and tactically managing other factors affecting perceived proximity can significantly compensate for the physical distance. An obvious way is to build a dense network where employees communicate and identify themselves with others naturally and in the right amount. Clearly defined roles and strong work culture would leave less room for uncertainty even in distributed groups.

Most companies are already embarking on the journey of digital transformation and can simply include the idea of providing additional structural assurance to their employees through tools. Further research on perceived proximity can lead to many such important recommendations for employers as well as employees and help us cope with challenges posed by remote work.

Key takeaways

- Social psychology principles suggest that individuals living closer to each other are more likely to form relationships as compared to those who are further away
- Contradictory to our conventional wisdom, geographically distant co-workers sometimes feel even closer to each other than colleagues in the same office. This is due to 'perceived proximity'
- With remote working, since distance becomes irrelevant and the mode of communication is the same, the frequency, interactivity, and depth of the conversation impact your perception of how close you are to a colleague
- Communicating frequently about the project's progress and engaging in comprehensive conversations about the goals with team members leads to a sense of collectiveness
- Once the state of identification with others (through common interests, culture, experiences, and job expertise) and an impression of inclusion is achieved in a peer group, it becomes easier to understand and to become closer to each other because the sense of identification leads to positive attributions in absence of real data
- A closely-knit organizational network with stronger norms is conducive to improved and effective communication. It also allows the members to easily maintain relations which is even more crucial in virtual teams
- When the organization offers structural assurance to its employees in the form of safeguards, such as legal recourse and technological features, employees communicate freely
- Technology plays a key role in both building a stronger network structure and facilitating structural assurance
- Technologies such as open-source infrastructure make collaboration easier and more transparent.

Food for thought

- In your context, how much of your work is – or could be – done remotely with other colleagues? What do you feel are the benefits and drawbacks of this?
- Think of the professional colleagues you get on well with. To what extent have your positive relationships with these people been

developed from face-to-face or remote communication? What elements brought you together?

- The pandemic, lockdown, and remote working/studying brought about a dramatic shift for many people – in a professional or academic context. To what extent did it present a challenging change for you? If it did, why? And if it didn't, why?
- To what extent do you think national culture plays a role in successful remote working relationships? Are some cultures more comfortable with distance and technology than others? To what extent does your national culture bear on this?

Related research: Wilson, J. M., Boyer O'Leary, M., Metiu, A., & Jett, Q. R. (2008). *Perceived Proximity in Virtual Work: Explaining the Paradox of Far-but-Close. Organization Studies, 29(7), 979–1002. https://doi.org/10 .1177/0170840607083105*

Three out-of-this-world lessons for remote working
The NASA way

Tanusree Jain and Louis Brennan

Routines change and evolve the most during a crisis. In a year unlike any other, the one change which is most certainly here to stay after 2020 is remote working. We are still getting used to the idea of working from home – sometimes getting stuck with a productivity block, or at other times working beyond official work hours. While these behaviours seemed okay during the onset of the pandemic, they are not sustainable. Other challenges of this new norm include the overlap between personal and professional time and, in most cases, smaller, more confined workspaces.

In this research, Jain and Brennan study how astronauts manage their time and identify cues from their routine that can help employees not only adapt to, but also thrive in, a hybrid working model.

The secret lies in your daily routine

Having regular habits and a structured daily routine enables people to be more productive as it frees up their cognitive energy from recurring tasks and allows them to focus on more complex ones. Think of your typical work routine before the pandemic: taking a warm tea or coffee with your desk partner, water cooler chat with your team members, or discussing a rundown of important meetings with a colleague during the commute back from work. These habits, in a balanced amount, are essential to set the stage for you to have a collaborative and productive day at work.

Your work routine can include several small tasks that you enjoy doing regularly to get a sense of predictability and stability in your professional life. The shift to full remote work and even to a hybrid mode of working demands the creation of new routines to replace the older ones and support these changes.

In this insight, several routines, perfected by astronauts, are explored to see what we, as Earthbound beings, can borrow from their techniques.

DOI: 10.4324/9781003388685-9

Three 'out-of-this-world' lessons

What makes us draw parallels from a space project to our office work? With critical dependency on effective communication and a strong teamwork ethic, space missions are an accurate representation of a physically dispersed and disconnected working environment. And even though there's no one-size-fits-all solution to champion remote work, there are certain NASA practices that we can embrace to become better at it.

1. Restructure your routine

COVID-19 put a major dent in everyone's routines and helping your employees regulate them by manufacturing *zeitgebers* can help. *Zeitgebers* are external or environmental cues such as sunlight, social interaction, or alarm clocks that regulate our biological clock. Derived from German, the word '*zeitgeber*' literally translates to 'time-giver' (*zeit* means 'time,' and *geber* means 'giver'). These cues set the pace and rhythm of our days and affect our moods, emotions, productivity, and thus, performance outcomes. You can take a moment to look around your room and identify the *zeitgebers* in your working or living environment that trigger you to be more in sync with the 24-hour cycle.

One of the strongest cues that affect your rhythmic cycle is light. For example, when you get exposed to daylight or even blue light from your electronic devices at the wrong time of the day, it disrupts the quality of your sleep. And when these external cues change even more as they did during the pandemic, our circadian rhythms become significantly disrupted and take a toll on the person.

What better way to learn how to adapt to these changes than looking at astronauts' work ethics? They go on space missions in a confined physical environment for extended periods and constantly need to alter their *zeitgebers* because they cannot rely on natural sunlight when they witness as many as 16 sunrises and sunsets every day. Additionally, space teams deal with drastic changes in their eating patterns and reduced personal interactions which makes following a routine even more challenging.

With a routine as fragmented as theirs, astronauts have learned to be more in sync over time by manufacturing their own *zeitgebers* such as celebrating special occasions and organizing social activities. Something even as little as having a meal together or video calling their families and friends goes a long way in surviving long expeditions. Managers for space missions also play an important role here to ensure that the performance of the astronauts does not get affected and that they meet their intermediate goals. For instance, mission managers break the overall goal of the space mission into smaller milestones. Not only does this help in tracking progress, but it also gives the astronauts a sense of achievement and motivation to keep going.

This practice is highly relevant to our current working context as a remote working structure becomes increasingly permanent. Just like astronauts, we must have rituals that help us develop a routine that works for us and help us adapt to the new normal. If you used to engage in casual interactions before starting work meetings in the office, make sure you do that even during virtual meetings. Alternatively, you can dedicate a specific time slot for 'no work' talks. It would help you to know your team members better, allowing you to collectively celebrate and appreciate the small wins that might go unnoticed because of the disconnected working environment.

2. *Managing freedom with discipline*

One implication of shifting from a physical to a virtual workplace that needs to be considered is how to balance flexibility with structure. More specifically, we must define how teams will be organised to facilitate collaboration. For instance, open working spaces seemed to work for many companies where ideas and conversations flowed organically. However, this idea of an agile working environment started to feel more like a pipedream when our physical interactions to a great extent became controlled and rigid.

Astronauts constantly struggle with this rigidity in their work and have found a way to overcome it. The solution lies in acknowledging and harnessing the power that lies within following a routine. While on space missions, astronauts stick to their schedule during weekdays and enjoy some flexibility over the weekends. We should also aim to strike such a balance in our hybrid working environment. Employees should be discouraged from working outside their work hours and encouraged to come to the office at least once or twice a week instead of going fully remote.

3. *See communication as your priority*

A manager calling to ask how their team members are doing and if they are facing any challenges is proven to deliver better outcomes than the one calling to ask why something is not up to the mark in the project. It is already well-established in organisations that internal communication among team members is crucial. But how we can reinstate the flow of communication after extended physical disconnection is something to think about. Moreover, as mentioned previously, not communicating enough with your colleagues regularly can be quite problematic when things go even slightly askew.

Related to this point is the importance of precision in communication. For astronauts, miscommunication has even proven to be lethal. In 2005, for example, an astronaut's life was almost lost during a spacewalk. Commander Leroy Chiao wandered into a new spot which was later discovered to be a hazardous area. The incident took place after a miscommunication between the ground controller office and the space crew about which handrail Chiao was on. Following this incident, NASA has worked closely with Russia to develop a set of clearer instructions and promote the usage of precise language to avoid future mishaps.

Having lived through a pandemic and subsequent lockdown, we might all agree that confinement and isolation trigger feelings of abandonment further. Indeed, astronauts tend to get hypersensitive during their space missions and, to help them with this challenge, NASA prioritizes regular check-ins with the team. Similarly, it is worthwhile for Earthbound managers to also factor in physical and verbal cues to develop bonds within the office and inculcate organisational values. With routine comes habit. And in the case of remote working and remote team management, this specific routine might end up saving, if not lives, at least morale and surely performance.

Key takeaways

- Having regular habits and a structured daily routine enables people to be more productive as it frees up their cognitive energy from recurring tasks and allows them to focus on more complex ones
- A work routine can include several small tasks that team members enjoy doing regularly to get a sense of predictability and stability in their professional lives
- The shift to full remote work and even to a hybrid mode of working demands the creation of new routines to replace the older ones and support these changes
- NASA's methods for their remote space teams include:
  - **Restructuring routines:** Use *zeitgebers* – external or environmental cues such as sunlight, social interaction, or alarm clocks that regulate our biological clock. Examples include: celebrating special occasions, team victories, organizing social activities, video check-ins, breaking the day into smaller milestones, casual interaction at the beginning of meetings, or alternative slots for 'no work' talks
  - **Managing freedom with discipline:** Balance flexibility with structure by ensuring that work is done during normal working hours and not beyond. Formalise rules by selecting in-office and home office workdays instead of fully remote working

- **Setting communication as a priority:** A manager calling to ask how their team members are doing and if they are facing any challenges is proven to deliver better outcomes than the one calling to ask why something is not up to the mark in the project. Not communicating enough with your colleagues regularly can be problematic when things go wrong. Be clear and precise in your communication. Be aware of hyper-sensitivity setting in among remote workers and temper this through regular team check-ins.

Food for thought

- To what extent does your routine help you to get through the remote working day and achieve results? What specific routine do you follow? How could you improve it?
- Make a list of all the *zeitgebers* you use (external or environmental cues such as sunlight, social interaction, or alarm clocks that regulate our biological clock). Which ones can you discard and what would you replace them with?
- How do you manage *your* online communication? How do your colleagues or peers react when you speak? What could you do to improve your communication during team or project virtual meetups?
- Draw up a list of 'lifelines' – the people you can rely on when things get tough during remote working. Who can you call or chat with for advice, reassurance, or simply a few minutes to chill out? Why would you choose these particular people?

Related research/work: What Space Missions Can Teach Us about Remote Work, MIT Management Review, November 16, 2021, Tanusree Jain and Louis Brennan.

Task bubbles and boosting remote project team success

Anca Metiu

War for talent

As technology becomes increasingly accessible, the competitive advantages between companies are blurred. To create a one-of-a-kind product or service is akin to discovering the eighth wonder of the world. Everything is about being incrementally better and infinitesimally more efficient. The message from the top firms is clear: we need you and we need you to do slightly better than what you did yesterday. In stark contrast to previous generations, the current generation of the workforce has the advantage of choosing who they want to work for and with. The War for Talent, as it is dubbed, is real and happening as we go about our daily lives.

For the current workforce, one of the deciding factors in choosing to work for a company is compatibility with the community and culture of the company. The candidate expects that there will be a healthy and positive atmosphere to work together and grow together with the company. Interestingly, this is a key expectation of the recruiters as well. Since technical skills have become standardized or can be taught, recruiters are increasingly hiring for softer skills, such as willingness to learn as well as how one can integrate and work within a team.

Miracles don't happen if you gather all the talented people of the world in a room. Recruiting them is one thing but creating a synergy between them so they can solve pressing problems is another. What dictates the efficiency of the group focus? How do individuals, as different as they come, come together for a common cause, and focus indefinitely to arrive at a solution? What are the factors that enable such collaboration? These are key questions that are relevant to all companies, irrespective of size, maturity, and industry since you seldom see a successful company run by a single person.

DOI: 10.4324/9781003388685-10

Micro processes for macro engagement

The group engagement process, defined by the mutual focus of attention of different people to achieve a common goal, is facilitated by three main micro-processes. This research found that the people involved in group engagement form a sort of imaginary bubble that keeps irrelevant stakeholders out so as not to disturb the flow of the process. This is the 'task bubble.' The members also use key artefacts such as a whiteboard or a computer screen to make the process intelligible to other members. And finally, there is shared emotion – which is both a motivating factor that keeps the fire burning and a result of the success of the process.

'Task bubbles' are imaginary bubbles formed around team members who are mutually focusing on a task at hand. These bubbles allow the members to achieve a state of *flow*, which psychologist Mihaly Csikszentmihalyi explains as 'a state in which people are so involved in an activity that nothing else seems to matter; the experience is so enjoyable that people will continue to do it even at great cost, for the sheer sake of doing it.' The 'task bubble' is porous so as to allow relevant stakeholders to enter it and make useful contributions to the task at hand and allow irrelevant stakeholders to exit quietly in order to not disturb the flow of the process.

Engaging in oral discussions for a prolonged period can be tiring, ineffective, and at times, boring. As such, the use of artefacts as support for thinking in solving the problem can be an effective way to sustain mutual focus for a longer period of time. When considering two groups solving a similar problem, the group that used task-related artefacts as part of their group engagement process fared considerably better than the group that chose not to use such artefacts.

As current, former, and future students may attest – even for a purely theoretical course, it is always better when the instructor uses artefacts such as a computer, a pointer, or even a whiteboard. It makes the transfer of information more cogent, holding the attention both of the communicator and the listener for a longer duration. The same argument can be extended to problem-solving processes in a company.

Shared emotion in the context of the group engagement process is a unique phenomenon contrary to the other two phenomena. It not only reinforces the mutual focus of attention in the group but is also an outcome of a successful collaboration of the group. In any task, and especially a complex one that involves multiple stakeholders, there needs to be a certain level of emotion involved to achieve progress and results.

This research demonstrates that a group that is emotionally invested in the problem (so much so that they are subconsciously thinking about it even when not in the office) performed substantially better than a group that views a task as just that – a task. Upon the successful completion of the process, the emotional reward for the group is high, unconsciously setting the need to repeat the pleasure experienced during the successful achievement of the task.

Catalysts of group engagement

The importance of having the micro processes in place to achieve group engagement has been strongly established. But are there any enablers who can help the group members in achieving group engagement? How can you propel the collaboration and focus among the team members? Indeed, there are several catalysts that help in creating the setting for the micro processes which in turn lead to the group engagement process. The enablers of the group engagement process function at various levels: *individual, interaction,* and *project.*

At the *individual* level, the enabling factor is the level of individual engagement. Indeed, how *individually* engaged, focused, and motivated the members of the group are is a key factor in achieving group engagement. Intuitively it makes sense to understand that a group of focused individuals can be easily engaged in a problem-solving exercise and are also more likely to achieve success compared to a group of torpid individuals. However, this research observed that individual engagement is a necessary, but not sufficient, condition for the group engagement process. It is only when these individual engagements lead to healthy interactions with others that the group engagement process is activated.

At the *interaction* level, there are two enabling factors: frequency and informality of interactions. As an analogy, Mozart is widely considered the greatest composer of all time, producing some of the most complex and popular tunes in the history of music. But a lesser-known fact is that he composed considerably more compositions than other composers of his time. For any creative process, including problem-solving, it is essential for the frequency of interactions to be high so that the probability of a breakthrough increases. Moreover, such frequent interactions would not produce breakthroughs if they were formal and monotonous. In this light, it is much better than to make these interactions informal to ensure that everyone has an opportunity to share their ideas without fear of being judged or crossing the line.

At the *project* level, it is imperative for work to take place in a compelling and visionary direction to effectively enable the group engagement process. Moreover, one of the key requirements of today's workforce is purpose in their work. *What effect is my work going to have on my immediate and future surroundings* is an increasingly asked question alongside those of working hours and salary. As such, the group engagement process benefits hugely from having a compelling *raison-d'être* that team members can relate to and work towards.

Focus on focus

Organisations spend tremendous amounts of money, time, and energy in providing resources and designing processes so that the workforce can focus on their tasks. Common approaches include motivating team members to work harder and collaboratively by clearly defining objectives, mitigating interpersonal conflicts among team members so that they can interact informally, and ensuring the periodic review of the team's progress and availability of any resources that teams might need to support them. However, all this is without value if individual engagement does not translate to group engagement, which in turn translates to the successful completion of the task at hand.

Hybrid work, combining workplace offices with work-from-home, is now increasingly the norm post-COVID-19. However, working remotely may represent a challenge to the group engagement process. And it is here that organisations can effectively focus on using micro-processes such as creating 'task bubbles,' ensuring the use of task-related artefacts, and ensuring a setting where shared emotion is easily developed between team members.

Key takeaways

- Miracles don't happen if you gather all the talented people of the world in a room. Recruiting them is one thing, but creating a synergy between them so they can solve pressing problems is another
- It is observed that the people involved in the group engagement form a sort of imaginary bubble that keeps irrelevant stakeholders out so as not to disturb the flow of the process
- The members also use key artefacts such as a whiteboard or a computer screen to make the process intelligible to other members
- Finally, there is a shared emotion which is both a motivating factor that keeps the fire burning and a result of the success of the process
- The enablers of group engagement process function at various levels - *individual, interaction,* and *project* levels
- At the *individual* level, the enabling factor is the level of individual engagement. How *individually* engaged, focused, and motivated

are the members of the group is a key factor in achieving group engagement

- At the *interaction* level, there are two enabling factors: frequency and informality of interactions. Higher the frequency and the more informal the interaction, the better the group engagement process
- At the *project* level, it is imperative that the work is in a compelling and visionary direction to enable the group engagement process. One of the key requirements of today's workforce is a purpose in their work.

Food for thought

- Think of a project you took part in with other colleagues or peers. Which factors led you to successfully complete the project? And to what extent did this success depend on the relationships built between the team members?
- To what extent was your last team meeting (or project meeting/studies group) 'facilitated' by the informal nature of it? Did the lead make use of any artefacts and if so, which? And how did s(he) use them?
- In your context, how would the creation of 'task bubbles' bring benefits to reaching your objectives or finishing your task? Which colleagues would you include in this "task bubble" and what implicit and explicit rules would exist to encourage success?

Related research*: Metiu, Anca, & Rothbard, Nancy P. (2013). Task Bubbles, Artifacts, Shared Emotion, and Mutual Focus of Attention: A Comparative Study of the Microprocesses of Group Engagement. Organisation Science, 24(2), 455–475. https://doi.org/10.1287/orsc.1120.0738*

Microcase

You are a senior manager of a large management consulting firm. Yes, *that* firm. You are preparing a short report to your boss, a partner of the firm, after the conclusion of a big project. This has possibly been the project of your life. The kind of project that makes or breaks a career. A large-scale study, committed by a major European port operator, about the future of that sector in the world. During this two-year project, you had to work with more than twenty experts, each of them located in different countries with few occasions to meet.

In this report, you need to explain how you managed these practical challenges. Some points you may want to raise:

- How to cope with time differences. One thing is to have a few hours' difference, but when you have a colleague in Los Angeles (Pacific Standard Time, UTC-8), another in Geneva (UTC+1) and the other one in Osaka (UTC+9), you will not be able to organize a meeting with all of them
- How to share information such as documents, recordings, and interview transcriptions
- How to prepare the report and prevent the risk of having different versions of the same document
- How to deal with different working styles. Some colleagues may prefer to work well in advance, while others only become active when the deadline approaches. In a face-to-face environment, one can see this easily, but how to deal with this issue online?
- Language: yes, language. We may speak good English or believe that we do. But we may still use local or regional expressions which are not easily understandable elsewhere. And in online meetings, accents can be another challenge. Even accents among native English speakers.

DOI: 10.4324/9781003388685-11

3 The influence of management, leadership, and organisational structure

Joana S.P. Story, Filipa Castanheira,
Beatriz Maria Braga,
Germano Glufke Reis, Jordi Trullen,
Veronica Casarin, Bernard Leca,
Stefan Linder, and Adrián Zicari

Committed companies
Do they create happier, higher-performing employees?

Joana S.P. Story and Filipa Castanheira

Corporate Social Responsibility – or CSR – emerged in the early 2000s, endorsed by reports from the OECD and EU and defined as the responsibility of enterprises for their impact on society. Broad in scope, CSR has since taken on other aspects, most notably sustainability, to include the need for a company to produce quality goods and services, reduce its environmental footprint, invest in employee training, ensure employee health and well-being, and maintain ethical and mutually beneficial relations with stakeholders.

With the objective in mind of measuring the effect of corporate commitments to Corporate Social Responsibility on employee performance, two types of CSR must be taken into account: external and internal. On the one hand, external CSR groups company activities aiming at environmental protection, community development, sustainable development, and corporate giving. Internal CSR, then, as the term suggests, looks inwards at the company's internal operations such as improving employee working conditions, encouraging mobility and career opportunities, establishing family-friendly initiatives, setting up training and development schemes, and implementing diversity and inclusion schemes.

CSR and employee performance: An indirect relationship through the mediation of job satisfaction?

Existing research has indeed established a link between the adoption of CSR policies by companies and the job satisfaction of their employees. This research insight drawn from the work of Joana S.P. Story and Filipa Castanheira goes a step further to analyse the impact of CSR on employee performance.

They take performance – the tasks and responsibilities for which an employee was taken on by an organisation in return for remuneration – and set it within the framework of social identity theory to explore whether both

DOI: 10.4324/9781003388685-13

external and internal CSR have a positive impact. Moreover, social identity theory in this context relates to how strong a connection the employee feels with his/her company. The logic behind this is that the more a firm engages in internal CSR actions, the greater the sense of identity an employee will feel for the firm, and therefore, give greater personal investment.

Following this, hypothetically, job satisfaction, or how much employees feel positive about their jobs and related tasks, should also affect performance. However, job satisfaction has other facets too that can be taken into account, not least because a job can be ambiguous in the effect it produces on the employee. Other influences can indirectly influence the level of satisfaction, such as esteem and positive emotions experienced within the company if colleagues show respect and recognise your role and results through being offered the opportunity to develop and achieve. It naturally follows that CSR perception plays a role in influencing job satisfaction.

In this respect, the greater the firm's CSR activity, both externally and internally – be it contributing to local communities or setting up career development training for its employees – the greater the job satisfaction employees will demonstrate. In this sense, job satisfaction would have a mediating effect on performance.

A third avenue to explore is the affective commitment employees might give to their company. Different from identifying with a company or finding job satisfaction, it expresses both the strength of an employee's identification with and commitment towards the organisation. Moreover, it's worth noting that the level of commitment has been found to stem from an employee's past and present work experiences, including the influences of geographical location, seniority, perceived skills and competence, salary, work ethics, and even the leadership style of senior management.

If the firm owns a high status and good reputation in wider society thanks to the quality and benefits it produces, here too there will be a tendency for an employee's commitment to be strengthened. The notion, then, is that the higher the CSR activity on the part of the organisation, both externally and internally, the greater the bond with and the more involved an employee will become in the company with a positive knock-on effect on job performance. As such, affective commitment should also act as a mediating factor.

The concrete impact of CSR commitments on employee performance

Surveying 190 supervisors and their subordinates in a reputed financial institution, also known for its effective CSR programme, Story and Castanheira's research produced unexpected results in relation to the effects of internal CSR commitments and the mediating effects of job satisfaction and affective commitment on employee performance.

First, it was found that there is a direct relationship between companies' external CSR commitments and employee performance. In other words, the more companies tend to have external CSR commitments, the more employee performance tends to increase. The effects of these commitments are the same on job satisfaction and the affective commitment of employees; the stronger these external CSR commitments are, the more these two feelings tend to increase. In addition, a partial mediation of job satisfaction between external CSR commitments and employee performance was found. In contrast, however, no mediating effect was found regarding affective commitment, thus refuting the supposition that greater levels of external company CSR boosted employee involvement within their organisations and job roles.

As for internal CSR, the study found a positive correlation between the degree of company commitment and affective commitment, as well as job satisfaction. However, internal CSR was found to have no direct impact on employee performance, with only job satisfaction demonstrating a meditating effect on employee performance. The lack of a direct relationship between internal CSR commitments and employee performance is surprising.

This would mean that although individuals may appreciate these practices, they do not feel that they trigger higher performance. Alternatively, it is also possible that employees do not see internal CSR as a motivator, but rather as a job satisfaction factor. As such, employee performance would not be particularly impacted by the company's internal CSR commitments, although they would feel more satisfied at work.

These results also indicate that companies' CSR commitments, whether internal or external, have a particular importance on job satisfaction, although the degree of impact on job satisfaction is not the same for external CSR as for internal CSR. In particular, external CSR has a much stronger impact on job satisfaction than internal CSR, although the relationship between internal CSR and job satisfaction is also very strong. In this light, these results corroborate previous studies on the subject according to which a stronger commitment by companies to CSR leads to higher employee satisfaction in the workplace.

Similarly, the affective commitment of employees tends to increase with companies' commitments to internal CSR. On the other hand, the impact of external CSR in this area, although it does exist, is much less. However, no link was found between employees' affective commitment and their job performance, whereas job satisfaction tends to increase their performance. The conclusion is that although CSR *as a whole* makes employees more committed to their organisations, employees feel that this attachment is stronger when organisations invest in them versus external stakeholders.

The impact on managers

From a more practical point of view, this study may be of particular interest to managers, as it highlights how important their company's commitments to CSR, particularly external CSR, are to employees.

First, they increase employee identification with the company in terms of affective commitment. Secondly, they lead to better performance at work. As for internal CSR, managers would be wise to understand that although internal CSR practices do not necessarily lead to higher performance, it doesn't mean that are not relevant or indeed important in the way a firm interacts with its workforce. On the one hand, the absence of internal commitments, even though the company is committed externally, could lead employees to think that their organisation is simply trying to improve its reputation. On the other hand, internal CSR commitments also make the company more attractive to future employees.

Key takeaways

- CSR encompasses the need for a company to produce quality goods and services, reduce its environmental footprint, invest in employee training, ensure employee health and well-being, and maintain ethical and mutually beneficial relations with stakeholders. These form two categories: internal CSR and external CSR
- Existing research has indeed established a link between the adoption of CSR policies by companies and the job satisfaction of their employees
- This research reveals a direct relationship between companies' external CSR commitments and employee performance; the more companies tend to have external CSR commitments, the more employee performance tends to increase
- A company's external CSR has a partial, mediating effect on employee job satisfaction and no effect on employee commitment
- Internal CSR initiatives were found to have a positive effect on both employee commitment and job satisfaction, but no direct impact on employee performance
- A company's CSR commitments, whether internal or external, have a particular importance on the job and employee satisfaction
- Although CSR *as a whole* makes employees more committed to their organisations, employees feel that this attachment is stronger when organisations invest in them versus external stakeholders.

Food for thought

- Think of your school, company, or organisation. What CSR-type initiatives does it conduct externally and for the benefit of wider society (helping local communities, partnerships with people with disabilities, job creation, environmental projects, fundraising, and charity, etc.)?
- What impact does this have on you as a member of, or student in, your organisation? In what way does it contribute to a positive mindset? To what extent does it change your behaviour in any way?
- How does your organisation directly or indirectly try to boost your motivation and commitment through internal CSR initiatives (for example, safe and comfortable working conditions, mentoring and/or career development sessions, modern facilities, recognition, etc.)? To what extent do they work?
- Name one thing you would like your school/company/organisation to do to improve your motivation and performance. What expected outcomes do you envisage?

Related research: *Corporate social responsibility and employee performance: Mediation role of job satisfaction and affective commitment, Corporate Social Responsibility and Environmental Management. J. S. P. Story, F. Castanheira, Wiley, https://doi.org/10.1002/csr.1752*

Does workplace authenticity count in attracting new talent?

Germano Glufke Reis, Beatriz Maria Braga, and Jordi Trullen

In normal circumstances choosing an employer – a company or organisation – is a hard task, full of comparison, doubt, reasoning, and introspection on one's real values, wants, and needs before committing to the employment contract. And, on the other side of the coin, attracting new talent is a hard task for an employer too. Today, the war for talent is fiercer than ever. Especially so after the disruption in working approaches caused by the COVID-19 pandemic and a marked shift in employee consciousness. Salary level, long hours, the race for recognition and promotion, or simply taking orders from others no longer necessarily form a healthy basis for true happiness.

In this context, research into workplace authenticity – the possibility to act and speak in line with one's values in the workplace – as a potential determining factor in attracting new talent offers both relevance and practical outcomes for companies and organisations. And not least their employer branding strategies.

Why workplace authenticity is important

Research on workplace authenticity is not new. However, previous studies have focused on authenticity as a primer for employee commitment, or the benefits authenticity brings to the company in terms of retaining and developing a more effective workforce. This research chooses to look at workplace authenticity through a new lens – that of exploring whether it could help attract new talent to firms, satisfy potential employees' growing desire for meaningful jobs and careers, and serve as an important factor to include in employer branding and recruitment drives. In a nutshell, Germano Glufke Reis, Beatriz Maria Braga, and Jordi Trullen argue that workplace authenticity may be taken into account – and given value to – by job applicants when selecting a future employer. Furthermore, they explore the importance of workplace authenticity in comparison to other, perhaps more traditional, factors of attractiveness for job seekers.

DOI: 10.4324/9781003388685-14

As such, the researchers conducted a survey among nearly 400 professionals in Brazil using two frameworks: the authentic living scale (Wood *et al.* 2008) and the employer attractiveness scale developed by Berthon, Ewing, and Hah (2005). The latter is interesting in that it allows us to compare workplace authenticity to other factors of employer attractiveness:

- An interesting, challenging, and stimulating job (interest value)
- A positive and pleasant social environment (social value)
- Above-average salary, security, and opportunities for promotion (economic value)
- Recognition and learning new skills (development value)
- Possibility to apply expertise and transmit knowledge (application value).

Adding workplace authenticity to the list, employees gave a score to each factor in terms of the importance of each factor when choosing a new job.

Employer attractiveness and the job seeker

Returning to the potential employee's job search, a key element in the list of decision-making criteria is that of the organisation's brand and reputation. Public image, prestige, or even innovative products or services may play a part. But conclusions based on what goes on inside the company – be it awards for best HR practice, word-of-mouth, employee turnover rate, or media coverage both good and bad – and subsequent weighing up of the pros and cons also count and increasingly so.

Indeed, prior research has pointed to both functional benefits for the job seeker (a good salary, interesting work environment, and mobility) and symbolic benefits that appeal more to an applicant's psychological need for freedom of expression and a positive self-image. That is, attributing human traits such as sincerity, cheerfulness, and an exciting atmosphere to the brand.

In that sense, the more positive a job seeker's beliefs are in a target organisation, the likelier (s)he will be attracted to it and commit to the task of updating, tailoring, and sending off a CV. For employers, knowing what their positive attributes are and how the job market perceives them is crucial for designing or re-adjusting their branding initiatives.

A dose of authenticity makes you more attractive

Much as good pay and career prospects add shine to a company and make it more appealing for the job seeker, so might the work environment if it fosters authentic behaviour among employees. Moreover, just as in any couple or any good relationship, we also look for similar values and behaviours, authenticity among them.

This is not only relevant once inside the organisation but it also has an impact on the recruitment and onboarding processes with research pointing to applicants obtaining more satisfying jobs when they are encouraged to express and portray themselves as they really are. Conversely, inauthentic behaviours in the workplace have been shown to negatively impact morale and motivation leading to decreased well-being and commitment to the organisation.

How does authenticity score against other employer attractiveness factors?

Reis, Braga, and Trullen's survey among 400 professionals in Brazil came up with some interesting and important findings for employers and employees alike. They were able to pinpoint results along several dimensions: gender, job level, and age.

- It was found that **women** give more importance to authenticity when applying for a job. Moreover, this is in line with existing work on gender roles, with women putting a priority on the natural and relational dimensions of work. These include the job itself, room for personal growth, the possibility to use creativity and knowledge in their organisation, and having good and friendly colleagues. This 'authentic way of living' – or should it be *working* – also increases over time among women when giving less of themselves to their children or ageing parents and seeking to nourish their own wants and needs
- Authenticity according to job level saw **top management** attributing the highest score for this factor of attractiveness. These were followed by employees in specialised job roles, middle management, line management, and lastly analysts, in that order. This importance given to authenticity is consistent with research carried out in 2011 by Michael W. Kraus et al. entitled 'The power to be me: power elevates self-concept consistency and authenticity.' (*Journal of Experimental Social Psychology*) Those higher up on the corporate ladder – and therefore with greater social power – tend to act more in line with their beliefs and values, seeking authenticity in their interactions and workplaces
- Finally, the survey results highlighted **age** as a differentiating factor. Older employees in the 43–65 age bracket gave authenticity a high score, mirroring the tendency to think less about financial reward and security and instead, focus more on social ties. Inversely, younger employees taking the survey were shown to give more importance to

having a 'good salary' and opportunities for promotion. This is not to say that younger people do not like good working relationships, indeed a good chat with good colleagues, but they tend to engage in social interaction primarily for information, networking, or advancement within the company. With the passage of time, however, comes age and with it a focus on the remaining time left for older employees and a subsequent shift towards catering to emotional needs, meaningful relationships, and maintaining their identity. As such, senior employees emphasise the present, not the future, seeking social links and workplaces where they can act naturally and in accordance with their values or how they see themselves to be – in short, authenticity.

More generally, Reis, Braga, and Trullen's research demonstrates that workplace authenticity is on a par with (in fact, slightly higher than) a good remuneration package and personal development in terms of employer attractiveness and significantly higher than either obtaining an interesting, challenging, and stimulating job; a positive and pleasant social environment; or the possibility to apply expertise and transmit knowledge. Very clearly, when looking for a new job, employees value being true to themselves and acting in line with their values.

How can firms capitalize on this?

One major takeaway for companies and organisations is proof that workplace authenticity counts both among employees and job seekers. In the tough war on talent mentioned at the beginning of this insight, firms can become more effective in attracting newbies by adapting their branding campaigns to put more emphasis on workplace authenticity. The possibility to act and express themselves in line with their values offers a much-need psychological benefit for employees, especially post-pandemic.

Firms' branding campaigns – pushed out through online platforms and social media – can benefit by featuring testimonials, online forums and chats, and employee blogs. This would enable applicants to interact with the actual people on the ground and glean precious information on how working for the company actually plays out on a day-to-day basis. As such, this presents a breath of fresh air from the countless generic content job seekers can come across that lauds a company's uniqueness, providing them with authentic 'face time' with real people and the organisation itself.

This is not without risk. Obviously, opening up employee banter on their working conditions and corporate environment might raise some quirks. However, it also plays in favour of the firm by playing on the transparency dimension – after all, you can't please everyone and criticism, however strong or unexpected, might be considered feedback in order to rectify and move on. Moreover, Reis, Braga, and Trullen's research seems to indicate that displaying both positive and negative employee comments does in fact increase a firm's chance of attracting better talent. For both the job seeker and the firm, authenticity offers light by easing the hard task of decision for the applicant and finding satisfaction. And by providing the opportunity to highlight a very meaningful criterion of the firm's appeal in a post-pandemic period characterised by increasingly choosy talent.

Key takeaways

- A key element in a job seeker's list of decision-making criteria to join a company is the organisation's brand and reputation. Public image, prestige, innovative products or services, awards for best HR practice, word-of-mouth, employee turnover rate, or media coverage are taken into account
- Prior research has pointed to both functional benefits for the job seeker – a good salary, interesting work environment, and mobility – and symbolic benefits that appeal more to an applicant's psychological need for freedom of expression and positive self-image: sincerity, cheerfulness, and exciting atmosphere to the brand
- The more positive a job seeker's beliefs are in a target organisation, the likelier (s)he will be attracted to it. For employers, knowing what their positive attributes are and how the job market perceives them, is crucial for designing or re-adjusting their branding initiatives
- In terms of employer attractiveness, workplace authenticity is significantly higher than obtaining an interesting, challenging, and stimulating job; a positive and pleasant social environment; or the possibility to apply expertise and transmit knowledge. When looking for a new job, employees value being true to themselves and acting in line with their values
- Women give more importance to authenticity when applying for a job. This increases over time among women when giving less of themselves to their children or ageing parents and seeking to nourish their own wants and needs
- Top management attributes the highest score for authenticity in a company. These were followed by employees in specialised job roles, middle management, line management, and lastly analysts, in that order. Employees with greater social power tend to act more in line with their beliefs and values, seeking authenticity in their interactions and workplaces
- Age is a differentiating factor. Older employees in the 43–65 age bracket gave authenticity a high score, mirroring the tendency to think less about financial reward and security, and instead, focus more on

social ties. Younger employees give more importance to having a 'good salary' and opportunities for promotion, using social ties primarily for information gathering and advancement in the organisation

- Firms can adapt their branding campaigns accordingly to put more emphasis on workplace authenticity. The possibility to act and express themselves in line with their values offers a much-need psychological benefit for employees, especially post-pandemic
- Firms' branding campaigns, pushed out through online platforms and social media, can benefit by featuring testimonials, online forums and chats, and employee blogs that reflect the firm's authenticity.

Food for thought

- Before reading this insight, what did you personally look for when applying for your current job? To what extent has that changed since and why?
- Take your own company, organisation, or higher education institution. How does it brand itself to appeal to potential talent or students?
- To what extent does this branding include the authenticity of the company, organisation, or higher education institution? How does it promote this dimension?
- Ask around you to different people based on gender, hierarchical position, or age on what attracts them to a new company/job. To what extent do their answers reflect the findings of this research?

Related research: *Reis, Germano Glufke, Braga, Beatriz Maria, & Trullen, Jordi. (2017). "Workplace Authenticity as an Attribute of Employer Attractiveness", Personnel Review, 46(8), 1962–1976. https://doi.org/10.1108/PR-07-2016-0156*

Berthon P., Ewing M., & Hah L. (2005). "Captivating Company: Dimensions of Attractiveness in Employer Branding", *International Journal of Advertising,* 24(2), 151–72.

Kraus, M.W., Chen, S., & Keltner, D. (2011). "The Power to be me: Power Elevates Self-Concept Consistency and Authenticity", *Journal of Experimental Social Psychology,* 47(5), 974–980.

Wood, A.M., Linley, A.P., Maltby, J., Baliousis, M., & Joseph, S. (2008). "The authentic Personality: A Theoretical and Empirical Conceptualization and the Development of the Authenticity Scale", *Journal of Counseling Psychology,* 55(3), 385–399.

Management control and stress

A double-edged sword

Veronica Casarin, Bernard Leca,
Stefan Linder, and Adrián Zicari

A salesperson at the end of the month struggles to achieve his sales quota. A store manager looks attentively at the expenses allowed in her budget. A young analyst prepares an internal report for the division director. In these three stories, one can see different systems – a sales objective, a budget, and an internal report. Each one of these tools is an example of a Management Control System (MCS) and nowadays these MCSs can be found everywhere in organisations. They are necessary to support the implementation of company objectives (the sales quota), track expenses (the budget), and monitor the operations of an area of the company (the internal report). MCSs are in every company, in every industrial sector, in any country. In a nutshell, they are commonplace in modern working life.

Design choices of management control systems (MCSs) can have a dramatic impact on employees' behaviour for good or for bad. What the Wells Fargo scandal taught us is that certain designs of MCSs, which, for example, base earn incentives on sales quotas, can encourage people to misbehave up to the point of engaging in escalating unethical and illegal practices, such as setting up bank accounts without customers' consent. In order to reduce the risk of such unethical behaviour, various scholars, writers, and business professionals have called for strengthening an ethical work climate and inviting (workers and) leaders to 'speak up' in order to bring ethical issues that they face to senior management's awareness.

This is undoubtedly important. Yet, it is not the full story. Those who design MCSs within an organisation *can* develop more awareness of the effects that MCS design choices have on employees and managers themselves. A well-designed set of MCSs can effectively help to set the ethical tone in the organisation. And it can help to avoid creating settings in which employees feel forced to cut corners or which imply harm to their health, e.g. experiencing burnout or stress-related health issues.

If the Wells Fargo scandal has put in the limelight the effects that MCSs can have on employees' behaviour, little attention so far has been paid to

DOI: 10.4324/9781003388685-15

the effects that MCSs can have on employees' well-being. A recent study by Casarin, Leca, Linder and Zicari at ESSEC Business School addresses this gap. Drawing from data collected among managers and employees in the UK and the US, the researchers identify the different features of MCSs that can increase the risk of harming employees. They particularly focus on job-related stress and burnout.

Stress: Both an ally and an enemy

We know stress. Chances are that each one of us suffers, at least occasionally, from it. Stress is a part of our hectic times. Many studies, in several countries, have clearly shown the human and economic consequences of stress and the toll it takes on the lives of people, families, and communities.

In their study, the researchers focus on job-related stress, that is, stress related to our working lives. They distinguish two dimensions of stress. Firstly, 'challenge stress,' which relates to an occasion to develop mastery and learn. For instance, you may now be reading this insight, perhaps making an effort to make sense of it, and (hopefully) getting inspired by it. This is 'challenge stress,' the spice of life, the positive kind of stress. It fosters performance. Yet, a situation can also trigger 'threat-related stress.' Anecdotally, in the aftermath of the Wells Fargo scandal, an employee reported that after working for the bank for a little more than a year he was experiencing physical reactions to the amount of stress he was under, due to the high sales performance culture in place at that point in the organisation.[1] This is a kind of stress, which typically does not result in productive thinking and work, but rather in some defensive actions and may imply health issues. Hence, in interest to spur performance and maintain well-being, responsible managers would want to keep it at bay.

Making management control systems ethical and beneficial

The researchers at ESSEC came up with four propositions for designing MCSs that do not harm employees. First, designers of MCSs should be careful about tight standards. For instance, increasing sales quotas while reducing resources would probably be a source of 'threat stress' for salespeople. Similarly, a continuously high workload and ambitious deadlines can also contribute to this type of stress. Second, a broad set of indicators, instead of a focus on financial indicators alone, could be beneficial. For instance, a combination of financial and non-financial indicators, as it is in the case of the balanced scorecard, can have positive implications in terms of stress, increasing the 'challenge stress' (the positive one) and diminishing the 'threat stress' (the problematic one). Third, remuneration systems may be designed in order to prevent 'threat stress.' More specifically, pay-for-performance schemes (compared to fixed salary schemes) would increase the level of 'challenge stress' while not having an impact on 'threat stress.'

These three principles are general ones and, as such, they can be put into practice in any MCS or any kind of company. After all, every company has some kind of planning system, a collection of indicators, and a remuneration policy. These universal MCSs which are inescapable in our modern lives, can be changed for the good. With the help of the aforementioned principles, companies can improve their existing tools, or design new ones that protect their employees by lowering 'threat stress,' while spurring effort and performance by providing them with challenges. Moreover, MCS tools can remain effective, without running the risk of harming employees. This ethical turn for MCS tools would be a welcome change, for companies and for each one of us.

Key takeaways

- Management Control Systems (MCS) can be designed to be ethical: appropriate designs will help firms develop the full potential of their employees by offering challenges without harming them by keeping 'threat stress' at bay
- MCSs should be careful about tight standards. For instance, increasing sales quotas while reducing resources would probably be a source of 'threat stress' for salespeople. Similarly, continuously high workloads and ambitious deadlines can also contribute to this type of stress
- A combination of financial and non-financial indicators, as is the case of the balanced scorecard, can increase 'challenge stress' (positive stress) and diminish 'threat stress' (negative)
- Pay-for-performance schemes (compared to fixed salary schemes) would increase 'challenge stress' while not impacting 'threat stress'
- An ethical reflection on the use of a MCS and its potential for bringing out the best in employees without harming them is a much-needed undertaking.

Food for thought

- Does your company or organisation have an ethics and compliance policy or management system in place? Why? Why not?
- To what extent do you agree that tight standards add to harmful job-related stress and burnout?

- And to what extent do you think that such standards are necessary in order to contain the risk of unethical behaviour and keep employees aware of the perils of a breach of conduct?
- If you are a more experienced employee, how do MCSs in your organisation look today and how did they look when you first started out in your career? What impact have the changes had on how managers and employees behave, their health and well-being, and on organisational performance?
- Is ethics necessary or the privilege of a developed few?

Note

1 Arnold, C. (2016). Former Wells Fargo Employees Describe Toxic Sales Culture, Even At HQ. *NPR Special Series*. Retrieved from https://www.npr.org/2016/10/04/496508361/former-wells-fargo-employees-describe-toxic-sales-culture-even-at-hq

Related research: Linder, S., Leca, B., Zicari, A., & Casarin, V. (2021). *Designing Ethical Management Control: Overcoming the Harmful Effect of Management Control Systems on Job-Related Stress. Journal of Business Ethics, 172(4), 747–764. https://doi.org/10.1007/s10551-020-04490-9*

Microcase

You are a young MBA student, just a few months before ending your program. Before doing this MBA, you had been working for a few years in a large bank in the Netherlands. Now that the program is ending, you have begun with job interviews. While some of your colleagues have already accepted a job offer, you remain sceptical. Yes, some of the companies are interesting. Yes, a few of them look promising. And yes, at least one of them will most probably send you a job offer.

However, you do not want to decide on a whim. You would want at least to have an idea of what matters to you, and which issues will be more or less important in your choice. For instance:

- Location: How far you would have to move? How cool will the city be?
- Travel: Would I need to travel a lot in my future job? Maybe I find travelling nice, maybe not so much
- Purpose: What does the company do? Is that a meaningful activity, something I can identify with?
- Contribution: How much can I help in that purpose? Granted, all work contributes in some sense, but perhaps I would like to contribute in some particular way
- Work environment: Is the company supportive, do they accompany their employees, and is it more or less competitive?
- Compensation: How big a salary do I need, expect, and desire?

Do you feel that this list is complete? If not, what would you like to add? From this list, which questions or issues would be a priority for you? Do you think these priorities will change later on for you, say in five or ten years from now?

DOI: 10.4324/9781003388685-16

4 Integrity as a driving notion for management and employees

*Na Fu, Peng He, Daniel Malan,
Ioana Lupu, Mayra Ruiz-Castro,
and Bernard Leca*

The manager's dilemma

Performance and the choice between treating team members equally or equitably

Na Fu

Being a line manager is no simple job. Motivating and enabling your team to perform well is crucial in reaching objectives and contributing to the long-term strategy, health, and results of your company or organisation. Dilemmas pop up every day and in many forms. Take the example of training. Do you offer a course in a key skill to all of your team members or those you have identified as high potential and high-performing? Which decision would cause satisfaction and motivation, or inversely dissatisfy and sour commitment further down the line? And to whom? The collective or the individual? The answer is not easy and forms something of a paradox.

Implementing human resource management practices

The skills, knowledge and output employees provide are an essential part of helping an organisation achieve a sustainable competitive advantage, and this is accentuated for firms working in the knowledge economy. As such, managing these employees and resources in an effective way through implementing HRM strategies is critical for the firm.

Typically, HRM – be it allocating resources, team composition, skills and training, or rewards, to name but a few – consists of *intended* HRM: that is, strategies created and developed by senior management for the organisation to employ to achieve optimal performance. However, what is intended is not necessarily *actual* HRM – what line managers in fact manage or choose to implement. A further dimension is added to the effectiveness of these strategies in the form of *perceived* HRM, which is how employees see and live these strategies.

It is here that the role of the line manager is key, acting as a type of hinge or interface between the intentions cascading down from top management to how team members actually perceive these and accordingly,

DOI: 10.4324/9781003388685-18

perform on the ground. This research from Na Fu et al. seeks to step back from previous studies which focused more on the *what* of HRM – the strategies themselves – to the *extent* to which line managers implement HRM strategies, *how* they do it, and *how* these managers' team members react as a result.

The extent or degree to which line managers implement HRM strategy is important in that many studies have indicated a positive correlation between this and firm performance or effectiveness. In the medium and long terms, it has been found to decrease staff turnover, improve job performance, and leads to more employee involvement in decision-making. Moreover, on a team level, the extent of implementation has also been found to lead to better outcomes – for example, an improvement in knowledge and skills, improved corporation between co-workers, win-win behaviours, and even what is termed greater *team viability* – that is, the potential for a team to stick together, work together, and achieve collective results.

But in addition to the extent of implementing HRM strategies, comes the dilemma of *how* to implement them. Should line managers think collectively and treat their resources equally and as a whole? Or should they treat their people equitably and as individuals?

Treating team members equally

So, how managers allocate resources and opportunities has an effect on their team members' perception, attitude, and behaviour towards the manager, team, and wider organisation. As the word 'team' suggests, it is a collective body of individual parts that form a whole. Treating these individuals equally seems to be a valid strategy to adopt. And when speaking of *equality*, then the word *consistency* may be linked to it. Indeed, research has shown that consistency – implying standard, same treatment across the board – is a powerful aspect of HRM implementation. Going further, the attributes of consistency include implementation that is free of bias, representative of the stakeholders concerned, and that is finally and importantly, continuously in line with ethical norms. And indeed, studies have shown that when jobs are interdependent, with each job function relying on others to achieve a result, treating your people equally boosts productivity.

However, consistency over time represents a challenge for line managers. Not only do they have to be constantly aware of senior management's *intended* HRM strategies as they are developed and pushed out through the organisation, but they also have to understand them – as well as consistently apply them on a daily basis.

If the manager gets it right, the benefits can be great. Consistency leads to alignment, and therefore effectiveness, with employees seeing a message that is clear, coherent, fair, and in line with their firm's values, procedures, and processes. Treating everyone equally also has the effect of snipping favouritism in the bud; the appearance of which can lead to feelings of unfairness and jealousy, not to mention a subsequent drop in motivation and future resistance to managerial initiatives. In short, equality strikes deep into people's perceptions of justice and leads to better collaboration between co-workers and team members.

The flip side of the coin, *inconsistency*, causes confusion and difficulty in understanding the legitimacy of HRM practices within the firm. Employees may counter this by opting out of the benefits and opportunities offered by the organisation; dissatisfaction and discontent; less engagement; and eventually, an increased wish to leave the organisation.

Treating team members equitably

The other side to the dilemma is focusing on the individual, and treating team members equitably. Here, the line manager is responsive to individual differences, in particular regarding team members' individual contributions and performance. The logic behind this is that individual team members can vary in the volume and quality of contributions to the whole – the team or company. And this is also an important dimension of line management implementation of HRM strategies. If a specific team member achieves great results, then it would only seem fair to reward this person in some way. And for individuals themselves, fairness to each one necessarily involves equitable sharing of recognition, resources, and opportunities.

High-potential employees, for example, are expected to be given more by their line managers than lower performers. This can come in the form of 'individual deals' with the team member regarding more flexible working hours and conditions, greater freedom, making an exception to individual needs, or even adjusting standard norms and procedures. The effect can be greater satisfaction with the line manager's implementation.

However, a red flag to raise would be that of the very difference between individuals – gender, culture, character, education, and work experience all serving to highlight an individual's difference and value – but at the same time highlighting the fact that these very differences might mean a different perception for each of what equitable treatment consists of. Would a bonus mean more to an older or younger employee, a modest or pushier employee? Would a female team member view customised coaching as greater recognition than specialised training?

Here again, previous research has shown that overall, when line managers implement HRM, equity helps individual team members to develop, serves as a catalyst for higher motivation, and in the end, produces better performance. It also leads to greater team viability and belief in the team's capacity to achieve good results.

Inversely, a lack of equity makes individual team members feel inadequately cared for by their managers. This, as is the case for the lack of equal treatment mentioned earlier, leads to dissatisfaction, decreased levels of motivation, and ultimately barriers to future performance.

As such, both treating employees equally and equitably have common benefits and outcomes as well as common drawbacks and negative outcomes. So, what for the delicately placed line manager who sits between top management and team member satisfaction: a happy or unhappy workforce and team results?

Going with the paradox

For the line manager, why not do both? On the surface, this might seem paradoxical. The very *raison d'être* of a wider system, an organisation, or a team naturally begs for collective action and the suppression of the individual for the benefit of the whole. But systems, organisations and teams actually work best when individuals identify with the whole and give the very best of their personal skills and strengths. This is the paradox. And indeed, this particular paradox is part of the leadership role. That is the leader's ability to treat her/his people uniformly while at the same time factoring in their individual identities, needs, and behaviours.

It can be complex. How to treat people equally by following norms institutionalised through processes and procedures, while taking into account individual cases and making exceptions to the rule? And how to also guarantee that sensitivities are reassured, and perceptions of fairness are maintained while doing it?

Here again, consistency is key. On a practical level, this means consistently implementing differential treatment – taking into account individual perceptions of equity – while keeping the wider processes and procedures as guiding threads regarding collective equality and organisational performance. Making adjustments for individuals also means ensuring that socially acceptable principles are understood by everyone; higher performance or contribution does indeed count as a justifiable reward for outstanding individual work.

By running these two, seemingly paradoxical approaches in parallel, employees will over time see them as a habit, a norm, and become less prone to feeling a sense of injustice or unfairness. Indeed, this 'new fairness' – a hybrid approach that takes into account both the collective need to treat people equally and the individual need to show equity and recognition – will most likely end up judged as practical and just. When implemented consistently by the line manager, and accepted by team members, individual differences will most probably lose their potential to create rivalry and feelings of unfairness. In essence, the team and its results remain important and an overriding goal while outstanding individuals are valued and respected by their peers within the team.

The win-win for team members, line manager, and organisation

Na Fu et al. point to the fact that their findings highlight the roles played by both *equal* and *equitable* treatment. Their study of line managers and team members within an international consulting firm leads them to conclude that both the degree of HRM strategy implementation and how these strategies are implemented, count for the team and corporate performance as well as organisational sustainability.

Moreover, the conclusion reached is that employing a simultaneous approach – that of differential treatment while emphasising common resources that all team members share – is highly effective both on an individual and collective dimension.

The practical outcomes are many. As mentioned at the beginning of this insight, line managers play a key role in generating the motivation for effective results and team longevity which in turn benefit the wider organisation and its financial well-being. Consistency plays an important part, both in implementing HRM practices – reminding team members of standard norms in terms of values, processes, procedures and behaviours – and highlighting the importance of recognising individual differences and rewards, especially for high performers.

These two simultaneous practices – equality and equity – enable managers to work through socially complex tensions, although it is no easy job to do. This is especially so given that most line managers are promoted to their positions through technical expertise and background, not through their people management skills. It is therefore important for them to receive training and support to ensure effective team management with an emphasis on balancing consistency with individual recognition. This being said, practices linked to effective HRM may be more easily employed by line managers than learning certain aspects of leadership such as inspiring through vision and purpose, or charismatic communication skills. After all, if the team perceives the line manager as fair and practical-minded in their approach to treatment, then performance and satisfaction will benefit without the need to make a seminal speech at every team meeting.

Fairness requires a common set of principles in dealing with all team members while at the same time respecting individual contributions. As such, a line manager has an interest in ensuring that her/his team members are aware of the benefits, processes and procedures the organisation offers employees. But also, an awareness that individuals are able to shine, and providing them with the possibility to obtain an '*i-deal*,' an idiosyncratic, personalised recognition of results and contribution to the team.

So, to return to the opening dilemma of offering training and the line manager's dilemma. Does the manager offer it to the many or to the few? In the paradoxical – let's say hybrid – approach to the issue, both equal and equitable is the answer; informing all team members of the purpose and opportunities for training while taking into account the individual contributions and probable benefits for each team member to attend.

Key takeaways

- The skills, knowledge and output employees provide are an essential part of helping an organisation achieve sustainable competitive advantage. Managing these employees and resources in an effective way through implementing HRM strategies is critical for the firm
- The role of the line manager is key in implementing HRM and how team members actually perceive these and accordingly perform
- Consistency leads to alignment, and therefore effectiveness, employees seeing a message that is clear, coherent, fair, and in line with their firm's values, procedures, and processes
- Treating everyone equally strikes deep into people's perceptions of justice and leads to better collaboration between co-workers and team members
- Inconsistency causes confusion and difficulty in understanding the legitimacy of HRM practices; dissatisfaction; less engagement; and an increased wish to leave the organisation
- Treating people equitably caters for individual differences, results, and contributions. It helps individual team members to develop, serves as a catalyst for higher motivation, and in the end run produces better performance. It also leads to greater team viability and belief in the team's capacity to reach good results and objectives
- Both treating employees *equally* and *equitably* have common benefits and outcomes as well as common drawbacks and negative outcomes. A paradox arises when suggesting that both approaches can be used simultaneously

- Consistency is also key in this case; consistently implementing differential treatment – taking into account individual perceptions of equity – while keeping the wider processes and procedures as guiding threads
- Making adjustments for individuals also means ensuring that socially acceptable principles are understood by everyone
- Line managers should ensure team members are aware of the benefits, processes, and procedures the organisation offers employees while offering the chance for individuals are able to shine with the possibility to obtain differential treatment and personalised recognition.

Food for thought

- Have you ever been in a situation where you felt injustice for making a great effort, achieving good results and not being recognised or rewarded for it? What emotions were triggered? Why did you feel them? To what extent were they linked to your values? And finally, did the event change your outlook on the degree of effort you gave after?
- How would you, as a newly appointed manager or future manager, drive your team? What three 'rules of the game' would you present to your team members in a first team meeting with them? To what extent has this research insight you have read contributed to those 'rules of the game?'
- What type of managerial style do you tend to appreciate most? A charismatic motivator who treats everyone equally? Or a pragmatic facilitator who prefers to treat individuals equitably? Think of a time when you were supervised by a manager or an instructor. What were their ways of treating team members or students? To what extent did you appreciate their approaches?

Related research: Line Managers as Paradox Navigators in HRM Implementation: Balancing Consistency and Individual Responsiveness; Na Fu; Patrick C. Flood; Denise M. Rousseau; Tim Morris. Journal of Management, 46(2), 203–233. https://doi.org/10.1177/0149206318785241

Leader integrity

How it influences the organisation and employee creativity

He Peng

Business integrity: Need of the hour

At this potential end stage of Capitalism 1.0, the business world still regularly faces scandals and ethical dilemmas, very often made public debate by the massive use of global social media.

What makes some companies avoid the temptation to act irresponsibly? By and large, it can be attributed to two main reasons: either they have a strong incentive to avoid facing media and legal backlash, or they have an innate sense of integrity built into their business model. While the incentive to dodge backlash is logical, integrity-based reasoning is naturally a more positive approach. In the extreme case of facing legal issues aside, there are many advantages for a firm acting in line with moral principles and likewise an abundance of consequences when it doesn't. Taking these two dimensions into account, the key problem lies in the intangibility of integrity. What is it? Indeed, we might have an understanding of it, but how can we formally define integrity, and more importantly, by what metrics can you measure it? The first step is to extend the integrity of the leader or top management to the integrity of the firm.

Leader integrity has not only been shown to prevent ethical dilemmas, but research and practice have also demonstrated that integrity is a key factor in ensuring leadership effectiveness, organisational behaviour, and business growth. Leader integrity is also contagious and cascades down through the firm resulting in positive employee attitudes and behaviours. It has been found that the perceived integrity of the leader is the single best predictor of trust for the workforce. And although not exclusively, the performance of the employee may also be a positive by-product of the leader's integrity.

On the flip side, and perhaps unsurprisingly, the lack of leader integrity has been shown to prompt negative employee behaviour. Lack of leader integrity is also touted to be a strong influencer in workforce absenteeism, consistent absence from work without good reason. The bottom line is that,

DOI: 10.4324/9781003388685-19

apart from the common understanding that integrity is a positive virtue, it also makes business sense to have leaders with integrity.

To what extent does leader integrity foster employee creativity?

Leader integrity has a significant impact on their organisations and employees. But can two seemingly unrelated phenomena – leader integrity and employee creativity – also be interdependent? This research by Peng He gives a resounding yes to the question. Leaders with a higher level of integrity indeed bring out a higher level of creativity in their employees than leaders with a lower level of integrity. And in order to understand this correlation, we need to look at integrity from two perspectives: the moral and the behavioural, since the definition of integrity depends largely on how employees view it.

From a moral perspective, integrity is viewed as a cumulation of being reliable, trustworthy, open, just, and empathetic. Reliability – or consistency in behaviour – is an essential part of leadership integrity since employees must believe that they will be rewarded when they make valuable contributions. It also encourages performance, helping team members feel safer taking risks since there is a high tolerance for mistakes or failures as long as processes are followed and employees learn from their mistakes. As for creativity, this can be considered a reciprocation mechanism or social exchange rule with the employee offering creativity and innovation in return for the leader's reliability. Trustworthiness too, plays a critical role, triggering more informal interactions in the workplace, which in turn leads to sharing information and coming up with new ideas. Finally, being open-minded, just, and empathetic are characteristics that can improve any ecosystem and the workplace is no exception – an open-minded leader is more likely to receive new ideas favourably and is less likely to hold a grudge in the case of contradiction. Ethical leaders also accept the risk of being criticised and the possibility that they too, may make mistakes. All in all, the above factors lead to an improved sense of belonging and a higher level of employee creativity.

From a behavioural perspective, integrity can be defined as consistency between the leader's words and actions, especially in the face of adversity. Humans are indeed hardwired to recognise and respect consistency between what others walk and talk about. And by practising what they preach, leaders set an example and send a clear message of what is valued in the firm's culture and what is not. Moreover, consistency also removes ambiguity in a company and offers a binary signal to any actions; either they are right, or they are wrong. From both perspectives, the message for leaders and firms is clear: recognise and reward integrity, and creativity will be a natural by-product.

'Monkey see, monkey do'

Given that leader integrity has overwhelmingly positive effects, how can integrity flow from top to bottom? As a natural human tendency, we like to reinforce our personal worldviews and biases by being associated with people with similar values. As a result, leaders with a higher level of integrity also naturally attract employees with a high level of sameness.

'*Monkey see, monkey do*' is a rudimentary, nevertheless accurate, rule of thumb for leaders setting and leading by example. Employees tend to mimic the social behaviour of people they admire and of people in power. So, when a leader exudes integrity, it also subconsciously instils integrity in employees. As we saw above, this integrity manifests itself as creativity when the opportunity arises.

However, employees view the influence of integrity differently, depending on where it stems from. For line managers and senior management – the C-suite – integrity has a different effect. Senior management integrity strongly influences the organisational *commitment* of the employee. The more integrity senior management possesses and demonstrates, the more an employee stays committed to the firm. Moreover, for Gen Z, who in the near future will constitute the majority of the workforce, a firm's integrity and values substantially determine their commitment to the organisation on a par with, or even more so, than the remuneration package on offer.

On the other hand, line manager integrity determines the organisational *behaviour* of the employees. This difference is primarily due to the fact that employees share most of their time and interactions with their L+1s and not with senior management. As a result, team members working under a manager with a high level of integrity will exhibit a more positive set of behaviours than those working under a manager with a low level of integrity.

Practice not preach

Lastly, a firm with a high degree of integrity, as virtuous as it sounds, also has substantial practical implications. To start at the grassroots level, managers and the HR function might do well to include integrity as an important criterion in the recruitment process of new employees. In addition, integrity could feature as a consideration for appraisal interviews, along with the setting up of regular training programmes to sensitise employees and improve integrity.

Although integrity throughout the organisation is important, the firm could also take exclusive initiatives to increase the appeal and importance of integrity at senior and top management levels. This special attention reflects the fact that it is senior management's influence that trickles down to other employees and which eventually shapes company culture. Highly focused training programmes in improving employees' professional ethical standards have deeper implications, and research suggests that in the event of a conflict between the corporate code of conduct and professional standards of conduct, employees often adhere to the latter for ultimate guidance. As such, firms would be wise to incorporate codes of ethics used by employees with employees' professional criteria.

Not too long ago, creativity, innovation, and critical thinking were not considered skills as such, very much relegated to the bottom of the list compared to hard skills such as programming language or the ability to carry out a P&L. Today, however, with technological advancement, they are among companies' most sought-after employee skills as 'thinking outside the box' becomes a game-changing factor in product innovation, market breakthrough, and business growth.

A cornerstone, and relatively easy-to-implement, strategy to improve employee creativity is for firms to hire or promote employees with a high level of integrity. Not only does it save the firm from the hazards of navigating through business scandals, but it also instils a positive and nurturing atmosphere where employees can exude confidence and ultimately, creativity.

Key takeaways

- Leader integrity helps to prevent ethical dilemmas and is a key factor in ensuring leadership effectiveness, organisational behaviour, and business growth
- In addition, this research shows that leaders with a higher level of integrity bring out a higher level of creativity in their employees than leaders with a lower level of integrity
- Integrity sets the environment for trust and openness, the possibility to learn from mistakes, risk-taking within processes, and creativity
- From a moral perspective, integrity is viewed as a cumulation of the following characteristics: reliability, trustworthiness, being open, just, and empathetic
- From a behavioural perspective, integrity is the consistency between the leader's words and actions, especially in the face of adversity
- '*Monkey see, monkey do*' is a rudimentary, nevertheless accurate, rule of thumb for leaders setting and leading by example. Employees tend

to mimic the social behaviour of people they admire and of people in power

- Not only does having high integrity save the firm from potential business scandals, but it also instils a positive and nurturing atmosphere where employees can exude confidence and creativity.

Food for thought

- Think of your own role and personality in what you do. To what extent is integrity a driving guideline for you? How do you put it into practice? What are the visible benefits?
- Many companies and organisations now have formalised codes of ethics or codes of conduct. However, this doesn't prevent corporate scandals from happening. Why?
- To what extent is integrity a universal value? Or should it be? Are there some cultures where integrity forms an innate part of behaviour? Why?
- Is there a limit to integrity? When might integrity be overstepped or made an exception – if ever?

Related research: Peng, H., & Wei, F. (2018). Trickle-Down Effects of Perceived Leader Integrity on Employee Creativity: A Moderated Mediation Model. *Journal of Business Ethics*, 150, 837–851. https://doi.org/10.1007/s10551-016-3226-3

Navigating ethical challenges

The strategic role of the Chief Integrity Officer

Daniel Malan

An increasing number of businesses are making conscious efforts to meet their long-term societal and environmental obligations. What makes this challenging and complicated is the fact that expectations have now changed radically compared to previous generations. Merely meeting the 'hard laws' is not enough to gain trust, and companies are frequently pushed to take a stance on social and even political issues. Leaving the risks involved in speaking up on controversial social matters aside, there are several other challenges in the way of an organisation's path to ethics and integrity.

As companies navigate towards an advanced digital era, new ethical challenges arise, such as the privacy and authenticity of their employees and customers. Employee activism in organisations has been on the rise and has increased even more so post-pandemic, with employees pressuring their companies to act proactively on issues that affect their well-being.

Indeed, companies are being held accountable for their environmental impact, philanthropy, working conditions, diversity, and inclusion, not least owing to the rise of transparency, reporting, and subsequent disclosure. An increasingly dense social media presence can take this even further by providing a platform for people to easily and openly share their ESG expectations, thereby mobilizing comments and opinions, sometimes on a massive scale.

The new role of the Chief Integrity Officer: Safeguarding ethics beyond compliance

Many organisations have realised that it's time for them to widen their approach to integrity by being more inclusive and strategic. Appointing a Chief Integrity Officer (CIO) to oversee the company's efforts and commitment towards integrity is one of the most observable steps taken by several organisations in recent times. As such, the primary responsibility of a CIO is to oversee the company's regulatory and integrity framework while creating an environment where employees can be happy and proud of the

DOI: 10.4324/9781003388685-20

meaningful contribution they make toward the company's overall vision. The CIO's role also includes providing insights into every key business discussion so that they act as a moral compass in the organisation's overall strategy and steer decisions toward the long-term benefit of the company.

Why the CIO role is important

In an organisation, CEOs often have to deal with complex decision-making processes when it comes to shaping corporate culture and delivering desirable near-term outcomes while playing in the long haul. More often than not, these long-term and short-term demands contradict each other. What further adds to this complexity is the difficulty in mapping a CEO's actions to the long-term achievements of a company. And even if CEOs make decisions that are beneficial for their company's future, it is often the case that results are achieved after their tenure is over. Consequently, CEOs may well end up opting for a short-term vision when it comes to making complex decisions. And this can sometimes lead to ethical misconduct.

Having a CIO in the organisation may well solve this issue to a great extent in the sense that they do not have profit and loss responsibility, thereby ensuring their commitment to integrity and an unbiased external perspective during important discussions. Moreover, it also guarantees that their integrity function remains independent from either financial reward or other pressures. In short, addressing integrity at the C-suite level not only provides the CIO with autonomy and legitimacy throughout the various levels of the organisation, but it also means that the integrity framework can be implemented to the totality of the organisation.

Driven by purpose and people, not profit

While the traditional and long-standing approach to running a company is centred around profit-making and expansion, in this research, the scenario calls for a more holistic approach to address integrity and ethical issues. It finds that senior management from various leading companies has been adopting a more comprehensive and strategic approach to conducting ethical business as opposed to the risk-based or legalistic approach focusing solely on punishments and enforced prevention.

A strategic approach suggests understanding the underlying reasons behind situations that do not comply with corporate policy or which pose a threat to the integrity of the organisation. Based on this approach, it becomes easier to nudge employees towards using their judgement and navigating through grey areas. Some organisations go further, seeking advice and support from external stakeholder councils or advisory boards.

To highlight the advantages of a holistic approach, we can witness Diversity, Equity, and Inclusion (DEI) as topics and initiatives that have gained momentum in the last few years. According to studies, organisations trying to tackle these issues in the firm by implementing tools such as zero-tolerance policies, performance ratings, and hiring requirements are actually *worsening* things instead of making conditions better. Why is that so? The reason lies in the fact that these attempts are developed to pre-empt lawsuits and not to address the issues directly. Research shows that strict law reinforcement can in fact result in fostering rebellion in a company and activating biases among employees even further.

On the other hand, some approaches have made strides in making workplaces more inclusive. Infusing diversity and inclusion throughout the organisation works better than one-off DEI initiatives or policies. Increased representation for minorities, mentoring programmes, and usage of more inclusive language in daily operations are some of the tactics that have historically proven to be more successful as compared to their risk prevention-based counterparts such as penalizing or imposing fines.

Making this strategic approach to integrity a reality: Emphasising the 'G' in ESG

Several factors need to be addressed if an organisation aims to minimize their negative corporate externalities on society using a strategic approach. The term ESG (short for environmental, social and governance) is a collection of evaluation criteria used to monitor and measure these factors and other responsible investment approaches. It helps in assessing the strength of an organisation's governance and the extent to which it manages the impacts of its social and environmental actions.

One key factor that is often overlooked is investing in solid governance in an organisation. Current reflection on governance often ends up simplifying it by discussing mainly compliance infrastructure, thereby missing out on the potential opportunity of having a deeper positive impact on organisational work culture and integrity.

Going further, governance holds a strategic advantage in ESG. Environmental and social commitments can be executed in a better and more efficient way by making conscious, strategic efforts to include the pillars of sustainability, ethics, and compliance across all departments.

Moreover, there are several ways in which organisations address integrity and ESG issues. Some can consider them to be an extension to risk management in the legal department, while others incorporate them into their supply chain or marketing campaigns. Taking the previous example of DEI, if a company is struggling with issues related to discrimination, the ethical culture of the organisation can readily be strengthened by utilising the support of its HR or people and culture teams.

The importance of a strategic approach through the Chief Integrity Officer role

Irrespective of the path taken, using a more holistic and strategic approach has indeed delivered desired, long-term outcomes for some leading companies included in this study. Novartis, a pharmaceutical and healthcare company, for example, announced a new and updated ethics code for its employees. The code centres around open-mindedness, honesty, and accountability and is accompanied by an interactive decision-making framework. It has proven effective, largely thanks to the method used to develop it. Instead of using a top-down approach and developing a code of ethics hallmarked by senior management, Novartis chose an inclusive approach, including the input from thousands of their employees to co-create it. Subsequently, this practice ensured that the principles included in the code were not only of significance to the employees but that employees would more willingly adhere to them since they contributed to its development. As a result, Novartis has witnessed a positive shift in employees' perception of ethics and compliance which further supports the adoption of a strategic approach to improve company culture.

At the end of the day, the evolution towards responsible and ethical management practices requires employers to remain on the pulse of their integrity commitments, with organisations no longer being able to underestimate the significance of ethics in the way they operate. The role of the Chief Integrity Officer, it seems, might just prove essential in that it provides a dedicated person, supported by a multidisciplinary team, strategically navigating organisational changes, coordinating throughout the company, and rendered legitimate through being attached directly to the senior decision-makers in the organisation.

Key takeaways

- Companies and organisations are increasingly being held accountable for their environmental impact, philanthropy, working conditions, diversity, and inclusion due to increased stakeholder pressure, transparency, reporting, disclosure, and social media that can make corporate misconduct a public debate
- Many organisations have realised that it is time for them to widen their approach to integrity by being more inclusive and strategic by appointing a Chief Integrity Officer (CIO) to oversee the company's efforts and commitment towards integrity

- In order for the CIO to have an impact and shape strategy, they must be attached to senior management and decision-making bodies, rely on multidisciplinarity teams, and practice autonomy while being removed from financial dimensions which might lead to favouring short-term vision and decisions
- A traditional compliance approach tends to be based on risk prevention through sanction which research shows to be detrimental to ethical behaviour among employees
- A strategic approach using integrity as a guiding thread suggests understanding the underlying reasons behind situations that do not comply with corporate policy or which pose a threat to the integrity of the organisation
- Integrity must become an innate feature of Governance in ESG, infusing through corporate layers and departments, and including employees in co-creation initiatives such as developing codes of ethics.

Food for thought

- As a potential investor or potential future employee of a company, to what extent would you investigate the company's footprint regarding its impact on the environment, the way in which it is governed, and its social impact? Why?
- Why should ethics and integrity be so important when commercial and civil law provides guidelines for companies to follow? What does integrity essentially impact?
- This research points to the appearance of the role of Chief Integrity Officer in some firms. To what extent do you think this role will be a common feature of companies and organisations in the future? Would you like your (future) career to go in this direction? Why, or why not?

Related research: World Economic Forum Partnering against Corruption Initiative (PACI) and Global Future Council on Transparency and Anti-Corruption: The Rise and Role of the Chief Integrity Officer: Leadership Imperatives in an ESG-Driven World. White paper, December 2021.

Long working hours and pressure from professional expectations

Is it time to change the habit?

Ioana Lupu, Mayra Ruiz-Castro,
and Bernard Leca

The time reads 7:00 pm. Up at six in the morning to clear away the mail and pave the way for a clear day of work on a key project, you breathe deeply, tasks completed. And just as you scroll the mouse to click the shutdown button on your computer, a pop-up from the project lead floats into the corner of your laptop.

Sorry to bother you. Urgent request from the boss. We'll have to stay late again – looks like we're in for a long haul. Can you do it?

You are an auditor in one of the big boutique firms. You're a professional. And this is how it goes. Pity for the evening out with your spouse. A quick call home. Then back to work.

Chances are that if you are indeed an auditor, a finance professional, an investment banker, a lawyer, or a surgeon you have experienced this. The problem is that today, many other jobs – from consultant to marketer to faculty member to advertising copywriter – are drawn into the cycle of what those in professional services firms call the norm. Why is this? And what, if at some point, you challenge this and decide to change?

Research from Ioana Lupu, Mayra Ruiz-Castro, and Bernard Leca attempts to answer these questions by focusing on the dynamics between long working hours and *role distancing*, the shift from professional expectations to a form of change – be it a redefinition of their role, a change in working conditions, or leaving their job.

The lot of the 'ideal worker'

Today, many firms and organisations expect their skilled professionals to take on an identity that centres on the 'ideal worker,' that is, putting in the hours (indeed, not counting them) with total commitment and availability for work-related tasks and events.

One of the issues with this is that modern professionals experience tensions and suffering between who they really are – their experienced identity

DOI: 10.4324/9781003388685-21

– and what they are expected to be and do in their working environment and roles. Employees caught in this dilemma resort to strategies to cope with it: humour, cynicism, *jouissance*, or rejecting their role or group identity entirely. Paradoxically however, previous research has found that despite these attempts to navigate excessive working conditions, employees become even more compliant and put off taking action that will free them from the constraints of their role and the organisation's practices.

Usually linked to high technical skills, expertise, and respect for strong work ethics, professional roles are particularly prone to long working hours. But being seen as a professional through others' expectations is more through the role they strive to meet as the 'ideal worker' and the subsequent behaviour they adopt than their level of technical expertise. Both management and supervision, together with socialising with peers in the organisation, tend to aggravate this penchant for long working hours with individuals being moulded to fit in or risk career obstacles if they do not comply. Indeed, responses recorded during this research pointed to excessive hours of work as 'the norm,' with departure from them seen to question the essence of being a 'true professional.' These practices become so anchored over time that professionals fail to see opportunities elsewhere or simply do not take them when they arise.

But, some professional workers do indeed challenge the norm and undergo changes in several ways. And this can become problematic, leading them to distance themselves from their established professional role, seek new definitions of themselves, and perhaps even leave – or be forced to leave – the organisation.

Role distancing

Little research has been made into why and how professionals can change their work practices and distance themselves from a professional role centred on long working hours. And this is in a context and despite many firms setting up various employee well-being and work-life balance initiatives; the professional services sector has failed to reduce the number of hours employees work or the high amount of burnouts.

The focus of Lupu, Ruiz-Castro, and Leca's research is two professional service firms (PSFs) in auditing and law, carrying out 75 interviews with mainly experienced staff with more than five years of experience. Typically, employees in these firms work over 50 hours per week with stints of 100 hours during busy periods. Junior professionals are resources allocated to projects, with little autonomy, required to travel at short notice, and working to tight deadlines. At the manager level upwards, roles change to advisory with more flexibility to work from home and tailor work around personal commitments such as family.

The concept of *role distancing* has been used to describe individuals who perform their expected social role but who display disdain and detachment from it. Within a company, such people make use of existing margins of manoeuvre to affirm a degree of independence from the role and its expected practices. In a way, it constitutes a signal of dissatisfaction and resistance – a deliberate non-identification with the professional role they have and an affirmation of their 'real selves' as compared to what they have to be at work.

Lupu, Ruiz-Castro, and Leca's new research on the subject disentangles the various facets of *role distancing* and explores its mechanisms further. It points to professionals distancing themselves by beginning to play their roles differently and making changes to institutionalised and implicit norms of behaviour such as working long hours. An emotional process, this distancing is usually accompanied by guilt, shame, or anger.

The research proposes a two-phase model of *role distancing*. The first process of *role apprehension* entails a shift in understanding, thinking, and emotions. It is in this first stage that workers begin to perceive their professional role as temporary and potentially changeable. Following this, a second stage in the role-distancing process is that of *role redefinition* where workers start modifying their work practices.

What triggers a change in mindset and attitude to your role?

Do you feel that your role and working practices are natural and unquestionable? If not, then you're experiencing *role apprehension* – the shift towards thinking that maybe what you're doing is only provisional and that change is possible. Research data from the interviews with professionals pointed to three factors triggering this change in attitude and mindset: *disruptive personal experiences*, *alternative socialization* (having experienced other ways of living and working prior to your present job and role), and *experiencing conflicting roles* between work and personal life.

Among employees questioning the norm of long working hours, some identified their change in attitude as originating from dramatic events or suffering occurring in their lives: the death of a loved one, miscarriage, divorce, burnout, or work-related depression. These events made them step back and think about what counted most in life – be it, family, couplehood, health, or happiness – and consequently, begin to question their excess commitment to long working hours with all the pressures it engendered. Moreover, times of crisis represent moments in life that trigger apprehension and force people to reflect on things previously taken for granted or accepted as normal.

Upbringing, family values, cultural values, and previous working experience in less restrictive environments ease the pivotal moment of beginning to question a current situation. A healthier work-life balance working in local government with shorter working days, for example, might have instilled values that clash with the 'ideal worker' role played within a more demanding and higher-paying job as a professional services provider, auditor, or consultant. One interviewee, struggling to cope with heavy workloads and long hours, kept her former routine of refusing to work on her days off or during the weekend. Amounting to a clash of cultures, her attitude was met with resistance by her team members who were unable to view their roles as anything but dedicated professionals, willing to put in the hours to reach delivery. Unwilling to change them, this particular manager was pushed to leave the company.

For other participants in the research interviews, their role distancing was triggered more by the fact of trying to balance their professional role with other meaningful roles in their private lives such as being a parent, an aspiring novelist, or even an active Christian. Mothers especially highlighted their former commitment and belief in their jobs before having a family; the tension and complexity in balancing the two once their baby was born pushed them to weigh up which meant most. In other cases, male employees experienced tensions due to their spouses' commitment to careers; although interestingly, a majority of males in senior positions with stay-at-home spouses did not experience the same tensions and were readier to accept and normalise the long working hours.

Yes, you can – no, I can't

Once the professional role is perceived as temporary and potentially changeable, both cognitive and emotional factors interweave to push the process further. Fundamentally, on a cognitive level, what happens is the very questioning of implicit or explicit rules or values at work which instil a sense of urgency and give onus to heavy workloads and tight deadlines. The employee, in short, begins to become aware of a sense of sacrifice that puts personal life at stake against professional. For some, it manifests itself in the realisation that their professional role isn't a matter of life or death, or saving the world. Or even a sense of the absurd: after all, why fix tight deadlines on such and such a day and time, when from experience the client will only probably consult the project days or weeks after the date? In short, the cognitive factor results in a kind of disengagement and disinterest in the game and its stakes such as reward, career advancement, or becoming – the icing on the cake – a partner in the firm.

Emotions kick in too, beginning with disenchantment. Resentment and bitterness may also occur, with professionals weighing up the important and essential in life with the time and commitment given to producing results. Which has more value? Time to live or time to work? After all, life is short.

But not short enough, it may seem. Lupu, Ruiz-Castro, and Leca's research also highlighted professionals' incapacity to think of change due to norms of working being so ingrained and institutionalised as to appear natural and inevitable. Indeed, understanding how work could be done differently without resorting to a 70-hour work week was at times a very lengthy process involving the 'un-learning' of habits anchored deep through contact with peers and mirroring leaders' behaviours.

For many interviewees, *role apprehension* was also an ephemeral occurrence, a reflection on *role distancing* ceding under the weight of normalised and institutionalised behaviours as employees returned to the status quo and normal run of things. Indeed, this short-term questioning of working customs may have constituted another natural need to vent and escape due to the pressures of working long hours. Nevertheless, many professionals returned to the known comfort of their old routines and the motivations of the game – prestige, reward, and career enhancement.

However, two factors stood out as game-changers leading to a more durable and intense dissatisfaction and apprehension: the accumulation of disruptive personal experiences and the intensity of emotions. With the subsequent effect of prompting employees to redefine their roles.

Get a life: Redefining your role

From *role apprehension* comes the second stage of *role redefinition*. Here, research findings point to two strategies used by professionals to gain control over their work-life balance.

The first – *private role redefinition* – consists in employees attempting to change their roles and working routine by themselves without trying to change the management or peer expectations of their professional roles. Invariably, employees sought to change their priorities: decreasing the importance given to commitment to work, setting up boundaries (such as decreasing or refusing to work on evenings, weekends or during their holidays), or –in a note of passive resistance – occasionally overlooking or ignoring requests for taking on new tasks and travel. These practices were considered 'unusual' for PSF environments, not without risk of sanction on behavioural or attitude reasons, and also providing only short-term relief for the incumbent.

A second strategy consisted of *public role redefinition*. Here, the employee attempts to change peer, manager, or workplace culture expectations – including working long hours – by resorting to company policy allowing for formal changes to work arrangements. Typically, these were flexitime schemes, for example, working from seven to four, or requesting a change of contract from full to part-time. Resorting to a public role redefinition naturally involves communicating the decision to peers and superiors. In the two firms under study, women were largely ahead in terms of attempting to redefine their job role – 54% compared to 33% male. The majority of these women also chose *public role redefinition* – 86% compared to only 15% of men. Indeed, a majority of male employees chose *private role redefinition*, offering temporary shifts in redefining the boundaries and scope of their jobs and working conditions.

In both cases – *private* and *public* – the researchers found that the attempts at redefining roles and expectations depended on two facilitating factors: work-related and personal. In the former, it was the availability of key resources and policies like HR professionals, internal mobility, or flexitime, and the support of the team, manager, and role models, those that had already changed or had experienced the *role distancing* processes, that helped. On the other hand, personal facilitators were identified as having flexible career ambitions – i.e., acceptance to give up on bonuses and lower career ambitions, seniority, and family work arrangements.

Indeed, seniority played an important role, often proving a major influencer in the ability to redefine roles. Not the least because their status enabled them to change without fear of negative consequences, but also because as seniors in the firm they possessed the privilege of flexibility and autonomy to tailor to a certain extent their working schedules and practices. Pity the poor junior though, whose intentions to redefine working expectations needed the green light of his superiors.

Personal situations also acted as a facilitator and more specifically, as mentioned above, family arrangements. Professionals, especially those in dual-career couples, benefitted from decreased risk by having a spouse earning a good salary. Inversely, employees in the traditional bread-winner role, or with stay-at-home spouses, found it more difficult to distance themselves from their traditional family role – only serving to strengthen their belief and commitment to the 'ideal worker,' professional role.

The wake-up call: Your choice

Back to that message you received at the beginning of this insight and the request to work through the evening. It's 7 pm but why not take it as a wake-up call? The choice is ultimately yours.

Let's look at the emotions involved. You may have felt slumped – rock bottom – at the thought of another evening spent working until midnight. You may have felt anger. You may have concluded that this was the final drop and the time had come to hand in your resignation. On the other hand, you may have felt a rush of adrenalin, a sense of challenge. Or even a sense of duty.

Perhaps, you're a dedicated professional, bound by your work ethic, corporate culture, and expectations to put in the extra mile. Fatigue and physical pains are of little importance as long as the job gets done properly and delivered on time. Perhaps it's ambition and career moves within the firm that spur you on.

Or maybe you've reached awareness. That something other than 150% commitment to the firm is important in your life – your newborn daughter, your family, your inner desire to write that bestselling novel. And just maybe, you're learning how to make a distinction between the two worlds of work and personal life and are thinking of saying 'Sorry – *no.*' In fact, you were just thinking of how to distance yourself a little from your professional role.

Role redefinition is a complex and challenging set of micro-processes that constitute something of a journey. It relies too on the support (or lack of it) of HR policies, flexibility within the firm, and also people within the firm that can lend a helping hand – colleagues or managers. These factors both shape the awareness and impact of the actions you might take to modify your working life – and, as role models in the case of colleagues and supervisors, trigger and strengthen *role apprehension* in others.

Key takeaways

- Many firms and organisations expect their skilled professionals to take on an identity that centres on the 'ideal worker' – long working hours, commitment, and availability for work-related tasks
- Modern professionals experience tensions and suffering between who they really are – their experienced identity – and what they are expected to be and do in their professional roles
- Peers, expectations, and firm culture make working long hours the norm with individuals risking career obstacles if they attempt to change this
- This research finds a two-phase model of role distancing: *role apprehension* (a shift in understanding, thinking and emotions that leads to viewing a professional role as temporary and changeable) followed in some cases by *role redefinition* (where workers modify their work practices)
- Three factors trigger role apprehension: *disruptive personal experiences*, *alternative socialization* (having experienced previous ways of working), and experiencing *conflicting roles* between work and personal life
- *Role apprehension* can be simply an ephemeral occurrence, professionals returning to their old routines and the motivations of the game – prestige, reward, and career enhancement

- But two factors lead to a more durable and intense dissatisfaction and apprehension: the accumulation of *disruptive personal experiences* and the intensity of emotions
- After *role apprehension* comes *role redefinition*. Employees use two strategies: *private role redefinition* (employees attempt to change their role and working routine by themselves); and *public role redefinition* (resorting to firm policy and initiatives for formal changes to work arrangements where communication of the change is required)
- Work-related (HR professionals, internal mobility, part-time contract, the support of the team, manager, and role models) and personal factors (dual career couples, children) facilitate the processes
- Seniority in the firm is a major influencer in the ability to redefine roles; status offers change without fear of negative consequences as does the privilege of senior position flexibility and autonomy to tailor their work practices.

Food for thought

- To what extent do you feel your company or organisation fosters or encourages the 'ideal worker' role? How?
- Some might say that employees should simply wear the mask of the 'ideal worker' during working hours and shut off once the working day is finished. How do you feel about this? Is it possible? Is it a thing of the past?
- If you were to realise that you were going through the *role-distancing* process, how would you deal with it? Would you internalize it, externalize it, attempt to change aspects of your job yourself, demand an official readjustment of your contract, or seek employment elsewhere? How do you justify the various decisions you make?
- In general, to what extent – post-pandemic – do you think prestige, reward, and career enhancement still be driving factors for your colleagues/peers? And what about you?
- How can employees and companies reach a win-win? What policies can be introduced? What explicit rules can replace the implicit? How to ensure that policies are followed?

Related research: Lupu, I., Ruiz-Castro, M., & Leca, B. (2022). *Role Distancing and the Persistence of Long Work Hours in Professional Service Firms. Organization Studies, 43(1), 7–33.* https://doi.org/10.1177/0170840620934064

Microcase

You recently came to País Libre, a small island state in the Caribbean. You are the local manager of SaveTheWorld (STW), a leading microfinance bank which has been in the country for some years now. Being a non-profit organisation, STW has the purpose of raising people out of poverty while achieving a moderate financial surplus which is always reinvested for expanding operations.

You now need to hire more credit officers. In STW, credit officers have a key role as they go to the countryside of País Libre, where most of the low-income people of the country live, and look for good candidates to receive micro-credits. There is a tension between giving more credits (as credit officers receive commissions for credits given) and making sure that the credits given remain low risk. Furthermore, the credit officer has to be a reliable person, as there is no way you can control this person on the ground. Whatever information she or he gives you, you have to take it as it is.

- How do you address this challenge?
- How would you design hiring, training, and evaluation practices around integrity?
- Which ideas would you put in place for monitoring integrity in such a context?

A further complication is how to evaluate credit officers. According to the mission of STW, you send credit officers everywhere on the island. But you very well know that some rural areas are richer than others – most notably the fertile plain close to the capital city, Santo Rosario. Obviously, credit officers there will have more opportunities to develop business compared to credit officers based elsewhere on the island.

DOI: 10.4324/9781003388685-22

- How can you make sure that all credit officers (those in the best area and those in the most difficult ones) have a fair deal?
- For those in poorer areas, how would you measure their performance?
- Would you think of other indicators beyond credits given as an indicator of organisational success in those areas?

You, this book, and your knowledge

1. How much did you know about the effects of the pandemic on working approaches, virtual work and team management approaches, and the role of integrity at work before reading this book?
   ❏ Very little ❏ Some notions ❏ Knowledgeable and eager to learn more ❏ I practise it

2. After reading this book, what three things will you most likely take away from it?...
....
....
....
....
....
....
....

3. Which insights in each chapter struck you most? Which were most useful? What knowledge will you most likely remember and take away with you for future use? ....
....
....
....
....
....
....
....

4. How much would you say about your understanding of responsible management practices and corporate responsibility now?

❑ Still very little, and I am still not convinced that companies and managers can be fully 'responsible' in nature and beneficial to their workforce given that performance and profit are the main drivers behind business

❑ I've learnt quite a bit and want to go deeper into the subject

❑ I've learnt a lot and I am convinced that this will shape both my career/career choice and approach to work.

How can you put this new knowledge into action?

❑ In one of my essay assignments

❑ As part of a student project I have been set

❑ As the subject of an article I will write for a blog or magazine

❑ In my internship, apprenticeship, or job

❑ I will show the book to my fellow students/work colleagues.

Index

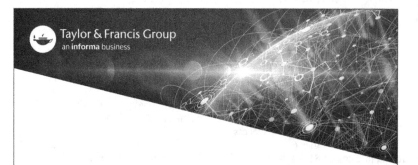

Printed in the United States
by Baker & Taylor Publisher Services